THE POWER OF
LOVE

*Wedding of Maria de Medici
and Henry IV of France*
by Jacopo da Empoli
See fig. 3.6, page 44

THE POWER OF
LOVE

JEWELS, ROMANCE AND ETERNITY

Beatriz Chadour-Sampson

UNICORN

This publication is partially funded with financial support
from Les Enluminures LTD and Benjamin Zucker

CONTENTS

Introduction

Love is the emblem of Eternity, it confounds all notion of time, effaces all memory of a beginning, all fear of an end: we fancy that we have always possessed what we love, so difficult is it to imagine how we could have lived without it.
(from *Corinne* by Germain de Stael, 1807)

LOVE IS A COMPLEX and powerful sensation which comes naturally and is almost impossible to define. It is uncontrollable; a subconscious and spontaneous feeling that overcomes us. Love is as old as civilisation. It transcends boundaries and cultures and is universally understood. Romantic love is an emotional attraction with a deep desire for togetherness, coming unexpectedly and without effort. Passionate love is characterised by intense emotions and sexual attraction. True love is unconditional, sharing affection, respecting and trusting one another, offering selfless and genuine companionship. There are many other forms: infatuation and obsessive love, illicit or adulterous love, love for family, and love in mourning for a lost beloved.

While love and romance remain timeless, jewellery expressing these sentiments has evolved and changed over time. Since its earliest beginnings, jewellery had been closely associated with the cycles of life and accompanied its wearers from cradle to grave, through birth, childhood, marriage and death. As early as 70,000 BC, prehistoric women wore decoratively strung sea shells as amuletic necklaces in hope of fertility, to conceive children and experience safe childbirth. Creating and raising a family belonged to the fundamental principles of the relationship between men and women.

Jewellery plays a central role in the history of love and marriage, given as tokens of affection to a loved one or to mark the union between two people. This book will provide an insight into how different cultures have interpreted love and how this is reflected in the choice and symbolism of love jewels through history. Some motifs are enduring; others may seem familiar but have evolved in meaning from one culture to another.

The emphasis of this book is on love jewellery from Western Europe, with a brief glimpse into the ancient civilisations which endowed us with many common

PREVIOUS PAGE
Cupid's Target
by François Boucher
See fig. 4.14, page 71

OPPOSITE
The Gresley Jewel
Miniatures by Nicholas Hilliard
See fig. 3.25b, page 58

surviving traditions. Love jewels reflect the diversity of the engagement ritual, dowries and presentation gifts involved in the wedding ceremony. The tradition of a ring being given as a sign of commitment goes back to Roman times, as does the joining of hands when taking the ceremonial vows of marriage. With the adoption of a Christian ceremony, the vows and covenant are made in a church and the union is blessed by a priest. The bridal couple promise faithfulness and trust when entering matrimony and the circular form of the ring is symbolic of eternal love, 'till death do us part'.

Throughout history, romantic love and the institution of marriage have been celebrated by the wearing of jewels. From the shell necklace to the heart pendant with diamonds, jewellers have been able to express some of our deepest emotions through their craftsmanship and imagination.

There is only one happiness in life, to love and be loved.
– George Sand

Ring with nuzzling doves perched on a nest by Ilgiz Fazulyanov
See fig. 6.28, page 122

OPPOSITE
Official engagement photograph of Prince William and Kate Middleton (future Duke and Duchess of Cambridge) with Diana, Princess of Wales' engagement ring
See fig. 6.42, page 130

1 The Ancient World
The Promise of Marriage

ENGAGEMENTS, DOWRIES, MARRIAGE CONTRACTS and commitment to marriage by taking a vow during a ceremony are all practices we associate with modern times but can be traced back to the earliest civilisations. The Sumerians in ancient Mesopotamia not only followed these customs and rites, but also recorded the law and code of behaviour. Prenuptial agreements were integral to the process, as are attested by surviving 4,000-year-old clay tablets written in cuneiform script. Some tablets specify the recommended bridal gifts, which were chiefly food and drink, oil, domestic utensils and personal belongings such as clothes, a quantity of silver and (unspecified) jewellery. A necklace is mentioned in one of the oldest known love stories from around 4000 BC, that of Innana, the ancient Sumerian goddess of love, beauty, sex, desire and procreation. In the mythical story relating to her courtship with Dumuzi, a shepherd and later her husband, her brother Utu the Sun God asks her, 'His cream is good; his milk is good. Innana, marry Dumuzi. You who adorn yourself with the agate necklace of fertility, why are you unwilling?' Fertility necklaces were worn by Sumerian women who wished for a family and protection during childbearing, a tradition that can be traced back to prehistoric shell necklaces.

For ancient Egyptians, jewels acted as amulets rather than love tokens, and were decorated with symbols and images of their gods. The magic powers of the gods would accompany the wearer through life. The Egyptians were known for their extensive use of amulets in everyday life, and in keeping with their beliefs they hoped for continued existence in the afterlife. The heart as a metaphorical symbol of attachment, love and romance was a much later concept, but our perception of the heart as the centre of emotion goes back to the Egyptian culture. They believed it to be the home of the spirit and the bodily element of the soul, the originator of all feelings. Amulets in the form of hearts therefore played a vital role in protecting that organ, which was key to achieving happiness in the afterlife (fig. 1.1).

Wedding ceremonies do not appear to have been customary. The young couple would establish a home together and receive gifts from the groom or the bride's family which could be seen as a dowry. A happy marriage with many children was

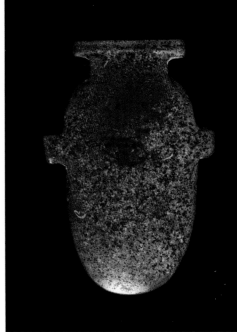

Fig. 1.1 ABOVE
Heart-shaped amulet
Ancient Egypt, New Kingdom,
18th Dynasty, 1550–1295 BC
Opaque red glass
British Museum, London

Fig. 1.2 OPPOSITE
**Red-figure Pelike (container)
with a marriage scene**
Greek, 4th century BC
Pottery
Staatliche Kunstsammlungen,
Dresden

the societal ideal, as they believed surviving children would nourish them in the afterlife. Women were known to have worn birth amulets depicting deities such as Bes and Tawaret, or Bastet. Love poems of the period reveal how Egyptian men had a high regard for women, with unconditional affection and love.

Jewels in the shape of scarabs (dung beetles), carved in stone or made of faience (glazed pottery) symbolised new life and regeneration. These were often engraved on the base and their powers enhanced by decoration or inscriptions. The pharaoh Amenhotep III (reigned 1386–49 BC) commissioned about 200 'marriage scarabs' to be distributed to the various provinces he ruled over. On the base, engraved in hieroglyphs, were his many achievements and an announcement of his marriage to the Great Royal Wife, Queen Tiye, along with a description of his many gifts to her, and the names of his other wives.

Jewels expressing love and desire through their design are first found in ancient Greece. Many of the wedding customs we know today have their origins in this period, such as the lifting of the bridal veil. As early as the 5th century BC, the secret marriage ceremony of Zeus and Hera from Greek mythology was depicted on reliefs (fig. 1.3). Here Zeus removes the bridal veil as a symbolic gesture. In real life, this act signified the conclusion of the wedding proceedings after three days of celebrations (fig. 1.2). These included the nuptial bath of the bride in perfumed water, the wedding feast and the following day when the bride was transferred to her husband's family. The marriage became legal once the couple lived together. The story of Zeus and Hera was celebrated throughout the Greek Empire and sculptures of Hera, known as the goddess of marriage, were adorned to look like a bride. An enchanting ring of the late 4th to early 3rd century BC refers to Hera as it sports an engraved goose on the bezel, one of her attributes (fig. 1.4). Geese were household animals but were also considered a symbol of love, alertness and a good wife. Images of Demeter, the goddess of agriculture and married women, can also be found engraved on rings or gemstones.

Hera's daughter was Aphrodite, the Greek goddess of love, beauty and desire. With her alluring appearance Aphrodite enticed the gods and men into illicit affairs. She was the mother of Eros, the god of love, a name we associate today with the word erotic. Goldsmiths and jewellers were fascinated by the stories and imagery surrounding these figures and crafted intricate jewels of love incorporating these subjects. In ancient Greece, jewellery was worn chiefly by women and ostentatious ornaments such as elaborate gold earrings would have drawn attention. The message could be unmistakable, as seen on a pair of large earrings from 330–300 BC with decoratively dangling Eros figures. In the centre of the design stands Nike, the goddess of victory, who was regarded as a matchmaker and maid of honour (fig. 1.5).

Fig. 1.5 LEFT
Pair of earrings with figures holding magic love charms
From treasure excavated in Kyme, Turkey (formerly Asia Minor)
Greek, c. 330–300 BC
Gold
British Museum, London

Fig. 1.6 BELOW
Ring with Aphrodite and Eros
Greek, 400–370 BC
Gold
British Museum, London

Fig. 1.7 BOTTOM
Ring with dancing Eros
Hellenistic Greece, 4th–3rd century BC
Gold
Musée du Louvre, Paris

Of all the female deities found on ancient Greek jewellery, Aphrodite was the most popular. On a Greek ring of the 4th century BC, a nude Aphrodite leans against a pillar with a bird on her hand, probably a sparrow which was sacred to her. She looks down to Eros holding a wreath, the emblem of victorious love (fig. 1.6). The image of the dancing Eros with all its sensual and erotic connotations became a favoured motif engraved on rings and gemstones (fig. 1.7).

Non-figurative motifs, such as the Heracles knot (a double knot created by two almost inseparable loops), were believed to have protective powers and evolved into wedding symbols. The knot may signify an unbreakable pledge but it is not known for sure if the phrase 'tying the knot' had its origins in classical antiquity. Jewels with Heracles knots were found in many forms, a favourite being simple gold rings made of twisted gold wires, but also in belts, diadems and bracelets, such as one example with inlaid gemstones, gold flowers and ivy foliage (fig. 1.8).

Ivy and grape vines were the attributes of Dionysus (later known as the Roman god Bacchus), the god of wine and fertility, who was commonly depicted holding a staff with a pine cone finial. The erotic connotations of the pine cone would later be revived in Renaissance jewels.

Many writers of the period describe how ancient Roman ladies loved their jewels. Jewellery was available to a wider spectrum of society than before. Greek jewellers were greatly admired for their skills and artistry, enjoying custom both in Rome and in the further outposts of the Empire. The Roman historian Livy (56 BC–AD17) describes the *Lex Oppia*, a law introduced in 215 BC to limit the weight of gold used in jewellery and the flaunting of luxury goods. However, enforcing the law proved impossible and it was abolished a mere twenty years later. The greater the wealth of the family, the more opulent the jewels on display. In his *Historiae Naturalis*, Pliny the Elder (AD 23–29) accused Lollia Paulina, a wealthy Roman noble lady and later consort of the Emperor Caligula, of being overdressed for an 'ordinary betrothal banquet'. She was laden with jewels, 'covered with emeralds and pearls interlaced alternately and shining all over her head, hair, ears, neck and fingers, the sum total amounting to the value of 40,000,000 sesterces'. A Roman woman's social standing was measured by the amount of jewellery included in her dowry. Family heirlooms were passed down from one generation to the next. Jewels kept their value and for the wife it was a form of insurance, should she be widowed or divorced. For the husband, the size of his bride's dowry could influence or even determine his future position in society.

Fig. 1.8
Armband with Heracles knot
Hellenistic Greece,
3rd–2nd century BC
Gold, garnets, emeralds, enamel
Metropolitan Museum of Art,
New York

The Romans introduced many new rituals still associated with marriage, including carrying the bride over the threshold, stag parties and formalised divorce. However, the most significant contribution which can be traced back to Roman culture is the giving of a betrothal or wedding ring, as a promise of marriage. The significance of the betrothal ring was comparable with today's engagement ring, as it was given by the prospective husband as a sign of commitment after the families had agreed all terms for the forthcoming wedding.

According to Roman tradition the bride-to-be was in the custody of the eldest male in the family, the *pater familias*. After he had given consent, the family of the bride would agree the terms of the union, the wording of the marriage contract and value of the dowry. The symbolic gift of the ring was insurance that the husband-to-be would keep his promise to marry the bride.

The designs of some Roman rings appear familiar to the modern world. One of these is the joining of right hands, a part of the betrothal ceremony known as *dextrarum iunctio* (fig. 1.9). The rings were made from either gold or silver, depending on the giver's means. A gold ring with a finely cut cameo showing the motif and the inscription 'OMONOIA', meaning unity, would have been given by a prosperous family (fig. 1.10).

The right hand was considered to be sacred to Fides, the goddess of trust and good faith. The clasping of the right hands of a betrothed couple was a gesture of loyalty and mutual agreement, usually representing concord at the conclusion of a contract. For the Romans this took place during the period of engagement after the families of bride and bridegroom had agreed on the terms of the proposed marriage and had exchanged gifts. The *dextrarum iunctio* was not a formal wedding ceremony as we now know it but has evolved into the symbolic gesture of the union of the bride and bridegroom during the modern wedding service. The design would remain a popular motif on betrothal or wedding rings into the 20th century.

Prior to the marriage celebrations, a social gathering was held with wine, food and dancing rather than a ceremony. The prospective bride took part in the *donatio ante nuptias*, a ritual during which she would give her dolls and toys as offerings to Venus, the goddess of love, or to Diana, the goddess of childbirth and virginity. Young girls were given a *lunula* (crescent moon) pendant to wear on a chain to wish them fertility and success (fig. 1.11), while boys wore phallus pendants as a symbol of virility. Later in the Roman period, men and women wore a phallus amulet symbolising abundance, luck and wealth in their married life. The rituals of the bride preparing for

Fig. 1.9
Relief with goddess Vesta blessing a betrothed couple
Roman, 2nd century AD
Marble
British Museum, London

Fig. 1.10
Ring with clasped hands and Latin inscription 'OMONOIA' (unity)
Roman, 2nd century AD
Gold, onyx cameo
Alice and Louis Koch Collection in the Swiss National Museum, Zurich

Fig. 1.11
**Necklace with
crescent-shaped pendant**
Roman, 1ˢᵗ–3ʳᵈ century AD
Gold
Metropolitan Museum of Art,
New York

the wedding celebrations were quite extensive, with the focus on her hair and veil rather than on her dress (fig. 1.12). She would wear a wreath on her head consisting of herbal flowers, such as marjoram, verbena or myrtle. For the Greeks and Romans, myrtle was the plant of love and sacred to Aphrodite/Venus, a tradition that has survived in many cultures. At weddings of the British royal family, myrtle is still added to the bride's flower bouquet.

According to contemporary accounts, the earliest Roman betrothal rings were made of iron, copper or brass. The first mention in Roman literature of a ring given as a pledge of love can be found in the comedies of the playwright Plautus (254–c.185 BC). The 2nd-century Christian author Tertullian praises the ladies of earlier generations who wore simple iron rings to mark their engagement rather than the large vulgar gold rings of his time. According to Pliny the Elder, whose discourses on natural history included gemstones and jewellery, the bridegroom gave the bride

Fig. 1.12
The Aldobrandini Wedding Fresco, depicting preparatory rituals for a wedding ceremony
Roman, 1st century BC
Fresco painting
Biblioteca Apostolica Vaticana, Vatican City

Fig. 1.13 FAR LEFT
Ring with Latin inscription 'VENVS FORTVNA' (Venus as the personification of Luck)
Roman, 2nd century AD
Gold, red jasper intaglio
Alice and Louis Koch Collection in the Swiss National Museum, Zurich

Fig. 1.14 LEFT
Ring with Cupid leaning on a torch
Roman, 2nd century AD
Gold
Alice and Louis Koch Collection in the Swiss National Museum, Zurich

a gold ring to wear during the ceremony and at special events, but an iron ring was worn at home. There is little visual evidence to prove these accounts of more modest rings, but the messages on surviving gold and silver Roman betrothal rings variously bless the couple with good luck and good wishes, happiness, unity and prosperity. On a 2nd-century AD Roman ring with an engraved red jasper intaglio, the Latin inscription 'VENVS FORTVNA' wishes the wearer luck in love (fig. 1.13).

Other popular motifs were engraved images of the goddess Venus and her son Cupid, the Roman versions of Aphrodite and Eros. Venus was considered the goddess of love, sex, fertility and prosperity, all values connected with married life. Cupid was associated with desire, erotic love attraction and affection, and was also known as Amor. Cupid is usually depicted with wings and holding an arrow or torch, symbolising how love can wound and enflame. His many attributes include bees, riding a dolphin, playing the lyre or leaning on a torch, as seen on a 2nd-century AD gold ring (fig. 1.14). Cupid's arrow has its roots in Greek mythology and is still a recognisable emblem of love.

Fig. 1.15 BELOW
Snake rings
Roman, 1st century AD
Gold
Metropolitan Museum of Art, New York

Fig. 1.16 OPPOSITE
Ring with Latin inscription 'ACCIPE DVLCIS' (Take this sweetheart for many years)
Roman, 2nd–3rd century AD
Gold
British Museum, London

Fig. 1.17
Ring with key-shaped extension
and cameo with Greek inscription
'[MNH]MONEYE' (remember
[me])
Late Roman, 3rd–4th century AD
Gold, brown onyx cameo
Private Collection

Another popular motif frequently found on Roman love jewels is the serpent or snake, especially the *ouroborus*, the snake biting its own tail, which symbolises eternity or the endless cycles of life and death (fig. 1.15). In Roman jewellery design, the snake played many roles, foremost as an amulet against the Evil Eye. From biblical times the natural and regular shedding of a snake's skin was used as a metaphor for rebirth, fertility or continual renewal of life. The snake was also associated with Venus and Bacchus, the Roman god of wine and revelry, and given aphrodisiac connotations. Snakes on rings and on bracelets (often sported in pairs), were thought to have been worn by young women.

Key rings, usually made of bronze or other base metals, were quite widespread in the Roman world. These rings had a key component built into their design and were thought to be used to open a casket or chest where money, jewellery or even the marriage contract was kept. This tradition dated back to the early Roman agrarian society, when the mistress of the house took on the role of household management. By the 3rd and 4th centuries the key rings had lost their practical function and had become exceedingly ornate and made of gold. They usually included inscriptions bestowing good luck, such as 'utere felix', or messages for a loved one, for example 'Take this sweetheart for many years' (fig. 1.16). Unusual examples include a key ring with a cameo depicting a hand pinching an earlobe with the thumb and forefinger (fig. 1.17) and the Greek inscription '[MNH]MONEYE' (remember [me]).

Some messages on rings were less explicit, as seen on a delicate gold ring with a carnelian intaglio finely engraved with erotic connotations (fig. 1.18). A mouse is seen riding a biga (a two-horsed chariot) pulled by two cocks. The mouse was a symbol of Venus and the cocks of the god Mercury, who was associated with luck.

Fig. 1.18
Ring with mouse riding a biga
pulled by two cocks and Latin
inscription 'HAVE DVLCIS' (Hail
sweetheart)
Roman, 2nd–3rd century AD
Gold, burnt carnelian intaglio
Alice and Louis Koch Collection
in the Swiss National Museum,
Zurich

The scene is surrounded by the Latin inscription 'HAVE DULCIS' (Hail sweetheart). Such a ring may have been intended for a lover rather than a wife.

Diamonds were known in the ancient world but, unlike today, they were rarely used in jewellery. The earliest description of the diamond with its natural octahedral shaped crystal can be found in Pliny's *Historiae Naturalis*, where he dedicated a whole volume to the subject of gemstones. He acknowledges the tough and hard qualities of diamonds and notes that they were reserved only for select people of royal status. The earliest surviving examples of diamonds set in rings date to the 2nd and 3rd centuries AD, but little is known about the significance of this gemstone to Roman contemporaries, other than their rarity value (fig. 1.19).

Until recently, it was thought diamonds were first worn in betrothal or wedding rings in the late medieval period. A recent interpretation of a passage in *Satire* VI.136–160 by the Roman poet Juvenal (about 55–125 AD), may shed light on their status. Juvenal refers to a legendary diamond ring which once graced the finger of the 1st-century Jewish princess Berenice, given to her by King Herod Agrippa II, her brother and allegedly her incestuous lover. Perhaps diamond rings were associated with love earlier than had been thought.

Even though marriage and motherhood were fundamental institutions in Roman society, it was socially acceptable for a man to seek pleasure in extra-marital affairs, while the wife was expected to be faithful and chaste. Many Roman authors wrote about the indulgent love affairs between young men and their girlfriends, or between married men and their mistresses. Such stories were recorded in the 2nd century AD by the Roman poet Ovid (43 BC–AD 71/18) in his *Ars amatoria* (The Arts of Love). He describes the various phases of a relationship between a man and woman, giving advice to men on how to win a woman, how to treat her and how the woman should keep a man true to her. In Book II,15, Ovid writes:

> *Ring, to encircle my beautiful girl's finger,*
> *appreciated only in terms of the giver's love,*
> *go as a dear gift! Receiving you with glad heart,*
> *may she slide you straightaway over her knuckle:*
> *May you suit her as well as you suit me,*
> *and smoothly fit the right finger with your true band*
> *Off you go then little gift:*
> *show her that true loyalty comes with you!*

After the Roman Emperor Constantine the Great (AD 272–337) had legalised Christianity, and Emperor Theodosius (AD 347–395) had declared it to be the official religion of the Roman Empire, marriage rituals barely changed but gradually evolved into the Christian nuptial mass. What did change was the imagery on betrothal rings. Pagan gods were replaced with Christian iconography and, during the Late Roman period, the bridal couple was often engraved facing each other on the bezel of the ring (fig. 1.21).

Fig. 1.19
Ring set with natural octahedral diamond
Roman, 3rd–4th century AD
Gold, diamond
The Griffin Collection, on deposit, The Metropolitan Museum of Art, New York (L2015.73.4)

Fig. 1.20
Marriage belt with wedding scenes
Byzantine, 6th-7th century AD
Gold
Musée du Louvre, Paris

During the course of the 4th century, the Roman Empire was divided into a Western empire ruling from Rome and an Eastern empire (now commonly referred to as the Byzantine Empire) whose emperor was based in Constantinople (formerly Byzantium, now Istanbul). Byzantine jewellery became very elaborate and the betrothal or wedding ring more complex in its iconography. By the 7th century, the marriage ceremony is depicted on Byzantine rings, often with Christ shown joining the right hands of the couple in a gesture of blessing. The presence of accompanying saints on some examples suggest the ceremony took place in the holy Sanctuary of a church (fig. 1.22).

Similar scenes are found on Byzantine marriage belts of the 6th and 7th centuries, which were wedding gifts. Surviving examples consist of gold medallions linked together, showing either heads of saints or scenes with Christ as guardian over the union of the bridal couple (fig. 1.20). Some even have additional inscriptions wishing the couple good health or the grace of God. Christian iconography sometimes sits alongside earlier pagan gods and symbolism relating to the marriage. Belts worn by young women were associated with fertility as far back as the Bronze Age and were believed to have magical powers in childbirth. A Byzantine 6th-century silver ring decorated with the *dextrarum iunctio*, the symbolic joining of the right hands, shows a shift in symbolic representation during this period of transition into the medieval age. The hand gesture is framed by two laurel leaves, emblems for immortality and eternity and, in this context, a reminder of the marriage vow of fidelity (fig. 1.23).

Fig. 1.21
Ring with married couple and Latin inscription 'VIVATIS' (live)
Roman, 3rd–4th century AD
Gold
Private Collection

Fig. 1.22 FAR LEFT
Ring with Christ blessing a couple and Greek inscription 'OMONOIA' (unity)
Byzantine, 7th century AD
Gold, niello
Musée du Louvre, Paris

Fig. 1.23 LEFT
Marriage ring with clasped right hands
Byzantine, 6th century AD
Silver
Alice and Louis Koch Collection in the Swiss National Museum, Zurich

2 The Middle Ages
Courtly Love and Holy Matrimony

COURTLY LOVE, AN EXPRESSION COINED in the late 19th century by the French medievalist Gaston Paris, describes the concept of romantic love that flowered in the literature and music of European courts from around 1100. Tales, poems and songs celebrated an idealistic and noble form of love independent of church strictures and untainted by real life. These were moralised stories that explored such emotions as chivalry and gallantry, passion, desire, jealousy and unrequited love. The earliest accounts of courtly love date back to the troubadours entertaining princely courts around 1100 in Occitania (southern France) and to the minnesinger of southern Germany. Possibly inspired by Arabic poetry of the 9th and 10th centuries, newly translated in the West, French troubadours wrote songs about chivalric knights falling in love, the rescue of a princess in jeopardy, or male lovers serving their chosen Lady in an honest and honourable manner. Devotion and discipline towards a loved one was foremost. Love poems such as *The Romance of the Rose*, the *Romance of Tristan* and others concerning the courtly games of love offered codes of conduct for gentlemen, largely based on the concept of chivalry. With the predominance of arranged marriages between noble families, courtly love provided a romantic and escapist way of rising above the formal constraints of life.

The increasingly popular literature and poetry on love influenced jewellery design. From the 13th century, the allegories of courtly love were depicted in manuscripts and on other luxury items: ivory combs and mirror cases, and caskets and jewels intricately crafted from gold and silver, materials only affordable to the highest classes of society. All over Europe sumptuary laws were introduced to restrict the use of gemstones, gold, silver and pearls to royalty and nobility. They were a way of limiting the wealth and distinguishing the rights of the different social classes and ensuring the position of the reigning monarchs.

The original owner of a gold enamelled brooch made in France around 1400 would have been from the nobility. Crafted with a lavish use of sapphire and pearls, it is of the highest quality and workmanship, showing a courtly lady dressed in a white and gold gown holding the heart of her lover in one hand and, in the other, a falcon (fig. 2.1). It is suffused with symbolism: she is surrounded by

OPPOSITE
Portrait of Lysbeth van Duvenvoirde
by anonymous painter
See fig. 2.10, page 32

Fig. 2.1
Brooch with a lady and falcon
Burgundy or Paris, 1400-30
Gold, enamel
Kunstgewerbemuseum, Staatliche
Museen zu Berlin

Fig. 2.2
The author and his beloved with a falcon, from the Codex Manesse by Konrad von Altstetten
Upper Rhine, c. 1300
Paint and ink on parchment
University of Heidelberg

Fig. 2.3 RIGHT
Love ring with lady holding a squirrel and French inscription '+ M(ON) AMOUR EST INFINITI(V)E DE VEU ESTRE SON RELATIFF' (My love is an infinitive which wants to be in the relative)
England or France, 15th century
Gold, sapphire
British Museum, London

Fig. 2.4 OPPOSITE
A knight offers his heart to a loved one
Arras (northern France), 15th century
Tapestry woven in wool and silk
Musée National du Moyen Âge et des Thermes de Cluny, Paris

small white flowers, probably myrtle and daisies representing love and beauty; the pearls represent chastity and the sapphire romantic love. Even the falcon is a metaphor for love, a device which also appears in the *Codex Manesse* (about 1300) by Konrad von Altenstetten, a minnesinger from the monastery of St Gallen in Switzerland. In an allegorical scene, von Altenstetten is depicted below his coat of arms embraced by a loved one and holding a falcon. The combination of this tableau with red roses in the background can be interpreted as a hunt for love (fig. 2.2).

Fabulous animals and mythical creatures were popular emblems of love in medieval art and literature. The dog occurs frequently as a symbol for loyalty. Small domestic animals kept as pets, such as rabbits and squirrels, represented love and devotion in stories and on luxury items given as love tokens. A rare depiction of a squirrel can be found on a gold ring of the late 14th to early 15th centuries (fig. 2.3). Engraved on the inside of the hoop, known only to wearer and giver, is a scene of a lady holding a pet squirrel on a lead accompanied by roses and carnations, its romantic intention emphasised by the loving inscription engraved in Latin around the outside. Roses were associated with Venus, the Roman goddess of love, evidence of the flowering of interest in classical mythology throughout Europe from the 14th century. Carnations stood for love and betrothal and the squirrel a metaphor for the devoted lover. The use of a valuable sapphire suggests the ring was given on a special occasion.

Similarly, on an early 15th-century tapestry from Arras, a knight offers his heart to a loved one. She sits on the left holding a falcon in her hand and at her feet a dog leaps up in friendship. The scene is surrounded by flowers and rabbits, all metaphors for loyalty, desire and romantic love (fig. 2.4).

Flowers and plants also acted as messengers of feelings, such as the oak tree and its distinctive leaves, which symbolised loyalty and constancy. On an English 15th-century gold posy ring (fig. 2.5), the exterior of the hoop is engraved with a frieze

Fig. 2.5
Ring with symbols of love and
French inscription
England, 15th century
Gold
Alice and Louis Koch Collection in
the Swiss National Museum, Zurich

of oak leaves and the interior with an inscription 'Loialte dort' (loyalty sleeps) or, from the French linguistic association between loyalty and dowry (love endows).

A recurring theme within the literature and songs of courtly love were the love tokens given by chivalric knights to the ladies they admired. These were often jewels, primarily the ring brooches, girdles and rings that were fashionable among contemporaries. Ring brooches were by far the most common type of brooch and were worn by men, women and children to fasten their tunics, gowns and cloaks. They were often engraved with messages of love, pious invocations or magical inscriptions. A frequently occurring inscription is 'Amor vincit omnia' (Love conquers all; fig. 2.6) from *Eclogue* X.69 by the Roman poet Virgil (70–59 BC).

In 'The Prioress's Tale', from *The Canterbury Tales* written around 1390 by English poet Geoffrey Chaucer (c. 1343–1400), the head of a fashionable convent known as Madame Eglantine (the wild rose) is eloquently described: 'her nun's habit is elegantly tailored, and she displays discreetly a little tasteful jewellery: a gold brooch on her rosary embossed with the nicely ambiguous Latin motto: Amor Vincit Omnia'.

While the culture of courtly love entertained the nobility of Europe with romanticised views of love and marriage, medieval church marriage customs were considerably more proscribed and restrictive. The early Christian theologian and philosopher Augustine of Hippo (354–430 AD) had written a treatise titled *On the Good of Marriage*. His views reflected church thinking across Christian Europe, with an emphasis on the holiness of the marriage sacrament and the indissolubility of the union. In this early medieval period wedding rituals still followed Roman traditions, but by the 12th century, attitudes and customs had shifted. With its increasing influence, the Church laid down strict rules concerning faith, morality and discipline. Social and cultural life was determined by the Church, as were all the rituals associated with rites of passage: birth, marriage and death.

Fig. 2.6
Ring brooch with love inscription
England, 14th century
Gold
British Museum, London

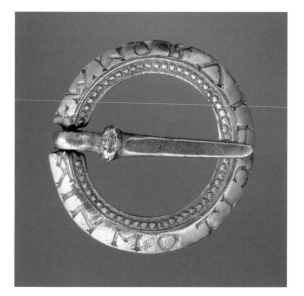

The wedding ceremony and the significance of the marriage rites changed after about 1100. Although multiple wives and divorce were commonplace in the Old Testament of the Bible, the medieval Church increasingly adopted the moral codes expounded in the New Testament based on the teachings of Christ. Adultery, divorce and remarrying was considered immoral. Humans were forbidden to divide what God had united. The stance of the Church was uncompromising and new rules were defined for believers and non-believers alike. Over the course of the medieval period, women progressively lost many rights of independence and property ownership, and were obliged to obey their husbands and become ever more dependent on them.

In choosing a partner, love was less of a deciding factor than before. Royal and aristocratic marriages were arranged by family elders often when the participants were very young, although they were not permitted to wed before reaching the age of twelve or thirteen. Liaisons were carefully decided on the principles of creating wealth and strengthening alliances for political reasons, territorial gain or even dynastic succession. Lower down the social scale, husbands and wives might be chosen by the individuals involved, but practical considerations still applied.

Before 1100 the wedding ceremony could take place outside any sacred area, and vows taken by the bridal couple were more of a symbolic commitment to the marriage. Over time, the Church became increasingly involved and the vows had to be exchanged in the presence of a priest. This would take place in front of the church door with the giving of a ring to the bride, as seen in a miniature painting of c. 1350 by Niccolò da Bologna (fig. 2.7). The scene shows the wedding celebration and, in a rare depiction, the actual bestowing of the ring with the bridegroom placing it on his bride's finger.

Fig. 2.7
The Marriage and the Kiss of the Bride by Niccolò di Giacomo da Bologna, from Johannes Andreae's *Novella* on the Decretals of Gregory IX
Italy, c. 1350
Miniature on vellum
Rosenwald Collection, National Gallery of Art, Washington DC

Following the official taking of the vows, a service would take place inside the Church and the priest would give his blessing to the married couple. The practice varied throughout Europe, depending on local traditions. In da Bologna's miniature a small vignette below the main scene shows the loving couple embracing with a kiss, a tradition still practised today. The bride is shown wearing her bridal crown.

Bridal crowns, coronals or less significant head jewels were often part of the bride's family dowry. They might also be part of the groom's family gift for the bride, along with a ring and sometimes other gold and silver items. In the anonymous treatise *Dives et Pauper*, dated around 1405–10, there is a description of what an English bride should be given when marrying:

> Thre ornaments logyn principally to a wife: a rynge on her finger, a broche on her breste and a garlonde on her hede, the ring betokenth true love … the broche cleannes in herte and chastity … the garlonde betokenth gladnesse and the dignitie of the sacrament of wedlocke.

For those who could not afford such a luxurious item as a bridal crown, some churches hired them out for the ceremony. The tradition may have originated from the ancient custom of placing a wreath on the bride's head. In many Western cultures the practice of wearing a bridal crown, tiara or floral wreath continues today; a crown of marriage for the bride who is 'Queen for the day' whatever her social rank.

In the medieval period, the bridal crown was foremost a statement of status. In 1402, Princess Blanche (1392–1409), the daughter of Henry IV of England, married

Fig. 2.8
The bridal crown of Princess Blanche
England or France, c. 1370–80
Gold, enamel, diamonds, emeralds,
rubies, sapphires, pearls
Schatzkammer der Residenz, Munich

Fig. 2.9
Jewish marriage ring
From the Erfurt Treasure
Germany, before 1349
Gold
Old Synagogue, Erfurt, Thuringia

Louis, son of Rupert of Germany, later Louis III, Elector Palatine of the Rhine (1378–1436). With her dowry she brought a magnificently bejewelled nuptial crown (fig. 2.8), originally made for Queen Anne of Bohemia when she married Richard II of England in 1382. It is a rare survival and the gemstones – rubies, sapphires, emeralds and pearl clusters – are symbolic not only of love and commitment, but also wealth and high status. It is not known if the crown was made in Bohemia, France or England, as designs for jewellery were often international. Goldsmiths travelled from one country to another working at the different courts of Europe.

A rare and exceptional early 14th-century Jewish marriage ring was discovered as part of the Erfurt Treasure (fig. 2.9), a hoard of goldsmiths' work, coins and jewellery found in 1998 in the wall of a medieval house in Erfurt, Germany. It was

Fig. 2.10
Portrait of Lysbeth van Duvenvoirde
by anonymous painter
Netherlandish, c. 1430
Oil on parchment
Rijksmuseum, Amsterdam

Fig. 2.11
**Belt-buckle with coat of arms
and couple**
Italy, 15th century
Silver, partially gilt, niello
British Museum, London

probably buried at a time when Jews were forced to disperse throughout Europe
after being blamed for the devastating outbreak of plague in Europe. According to
Jewish rituals, the marriage ring was only worn for ceremonial purposes during
the wedding ceremony, and the use of gemstones was not permitted. Interestingly,
although the ring is plain gold in accordance with religious regulations, the style is
Western European with fine Gothic tracery on the architectural bezel and the classical
motif of clasped hands hidden on the underside of the hoop. The architectural design
was probably more than just decorative. Although it is in keeping with the style
of architecture local to the goldsmith and the ring's owners, it also follows Jewish
traditions by symbolising the home and life of the married couple, according to the
vision of the Torah.

In the ancient world, young women were given belts to protect or encourage
fertility, and this sentiment persisted throughout the medieval period and even into
the Renaissance. In a well-documented, full-length portrait of around 1430, Lysbeth
van Duvenvoirde is depicted wearing a high-waisted gold belt inlaid with sapphires
around her fashionable long red huppelande dress (fig. 2.10). With her fingers she
holds a banderole or scroll bearing the Netherlandish inscription 'Mi verdriet lange
te hopen, Wie is hi di sijn hert hout open' (It saddens me to yearn so long. Who is
it that will open up his heart?). The portrait was originally accompanied by one of
Simone van Adrichem with the banderole reading 'I have been afeared. Who is it
that would honour my love.' The portraits were thought to have been painted on

the occasion of their marriage. The sapphires in her belt may represent romantic love, and the four bells, which were thought to ward off evil spirits, may symbolise protection of the marriage, or even safe pregnancy. An Italian belt buckle of the same period, made of silver with gilding and black niello decoration, depicts a couple facing each other on either side of an armorial shield and the initials L and B (fig. 2.11). These were probably the initials of the bridal couple's first names. Such an ornamental buckle would have been attached to an embroidered silk belt, possibly with imagery pertaining to love.

In medieval jewellery, sacred and secular worlds were often entwined, for example on ring brooches and finger rings featuring devotional images or messages invoking a saint for protection. 15th-century gold and silver 'iconographic rings' could have up to three engraved images of saints on the bezel and hoop of the ring. The chosen saints might relate to the name of the owner, be the patron saint of a specific profession, or, more often, might invoke special powers against illnesses or distresses in life. These are rarely found with a love inscription but a mid to late 15th-century example bears the motto 'mon cor avez' (have my heart) engraved inside the hoop, probably intended to remain secret (fig. 2.12). It depicts St John the Baptist and St Catherine flanking an image of the Virgin and Child in the centre. From the 12th century, the Virgin Mary was venerated with great piety as an icon of motherhood, and increasingly called upon by women. Perhaps the original owner was a mother expecting a child and seeking protection in childbirth.

More common in England were posy rings, their name deriving from the term *poesie* (poetry). These were plain gold bands with mottos or inscriptions in prose or verse, such as '+ *pense de moy*' (think of me; fig. 2.13). The love messages were either on the outside of the hoop to be seen and worn with pride or hidden inside the hoop and only known to the giver and recipient. The repeated use of particular verses suggests that goldsmiths and engravers had printed books providing a selection of examples to offer clients. Posy rings were given as a sign of friendship or love and continued to serve in the rites of betrothal or marriage beyond the medieval period, occasionally bearing Christian messages. The ring type would gain in significance as wedding bands in the following centuries.

Some symbolism survived from ancient Roman times. The clasped right hands, the *dextrarum iunctio*, continued into the medieval period and became known as the *fede* motif (from the Italian for trust or loyalty). The joining of the hands features twice on a 14th-century gold brooch and was a favoured motif on rings (fig. 2.14). An array of charming romantic declarations can be found on ring brooches of the period, such as 'IO SUI ICI EN LIU DAMI: AMO' (I am here in the place of the friend I love) on a 13th-century gold brooch with rubies and sapphires (fig. 2.15). Many such inscriptions on brooches and rings are in French, rarely Latin or English. French was the language of love and diplomacy, understood by the aristocracy and higher social classes who could afford such jewels. The

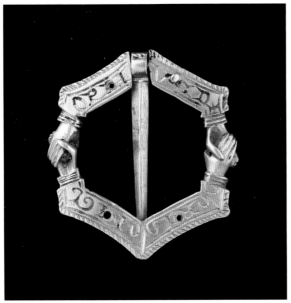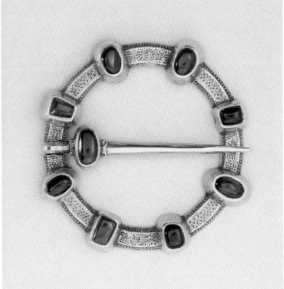

language used in these inscriptions, however, rarely pointed to where the piece was made or worn. Throughout the Middle Ages similar designs could be found all over Europe, spread by itinerant craftsmen and, later, through printed pattern books. The use of gemstones on these brooches, with their symbolic associations, would intensify the message. The rubies and sapphires would have been imported from Sri Lanka, Myanmar or even India and traded via Venice. During this period stones were not faceted but left in their natural, rounded shape, called cabochons, and simply polished.

The heart is a timeless and universal symbol of love on jewellery. A heart-shaped gold brooch with opaque white and blue enamel was found as part of the Fishpool Hoard, treasure dating to around 1400–64 which was discovered in Nottinghamshire, England, in 1966. On the reverse, the brooch bears the romantic inscription in French, 'Je suy vostre ans de partir' (I am yours forever) between stylised flowers, possibly myrtle (figs. 2.16a and b). Hidden on the back, unseen by the viewer, this dedication would have been shared only between the giver and wearer of this love token.

In contrast, a gold ring with heart-shaped bezel and ruby cabochon from 14th-century Italy has a message (fig. 2.17) openly inscribed along the outer part of the hoop: 'CORTE PORT [A] AMOR' (courtship/the heart brings love). The sentiment comes from Sonnet 36 by the Italian poet Guido Cavalcanti (1255–1300).

As it still does today, the padlock symbolised unbreakable love. Sweethearts now lock them to fences, bridges or gates, marked with initials, names or messages of love. In the medieval period, miniature padlocks were used as a motif on rings or as gold lockets, such as a 15th-century example found in the Fishpool Hoard (fig. 2.19).

Fig. 2.14 ABOVE, LEFT
Ring brooch with clasped right hands
France or England, 14th century
Gold, pearl
Musée National du Moyen Âge et des Thermes de Cluny, Paris

Fig. 2.15 ABOVE, RIGHT
Ring brooch with French inscription
France or England, 13th century
Gold, rubies, sapphires
British Museum, London

Fig. 2.16a and b
Heart-shaped ring brooch with French inscription (front and reverse)
From the Fishpool Hoard
England, c. 1400–64
Gold, enamel
British Museum, London

This was possibly originally intended as a fastener for a chain and may have had pearls suspended from it, denoting purity. This is underlined by the inscriptions on both sides which together read 'sauns repentir' (without regret) and the tiny white enamelled flowers, either myrtle or strawberry flowers, both associated with purity, sensuality and love.

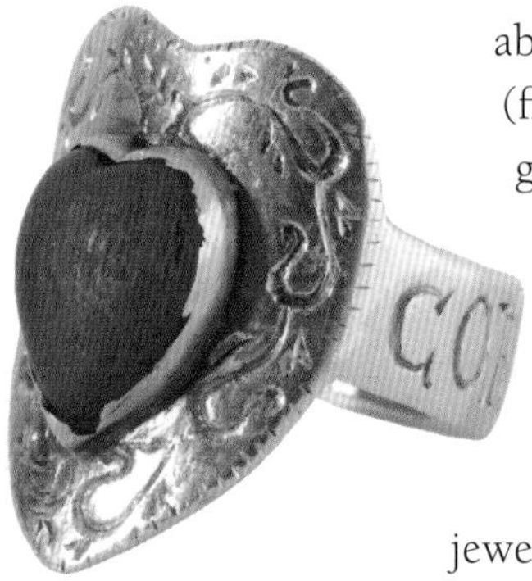

Gemstones became increasingly favoured in love jewels, not just for their beauty and value but also for their symbolic qualities. A superb Burgundian brooch of about 1430–40 boasts an exemplary choice of gems and finely sculpted figures (fig. 2.18). A young couple stand under a tree (now incomplete) within the garden of love, a common courtly conceit, defined by gold wire fencing and reminiscent of the wedding wreath. Between them is a triangular cut diamond symbolising virtue and constancy, alongside a ruby cabochon – the stone of love – and five pearls representing purity and chastity. The couple hold a green enamelled garland of mistletoe, which was believed to bestow life and fertility and even thought to be an aphrodisiac. This costly enamelled jewel would have once belonged to a member of the high nobility. It may have been passed down from Mary, Duchess of Burgundy (1457–82) and then by descent to her grandson the Holy Roman Emperor Ferdinand I (1503–64), in whose inventories it is first mentioned.

By the 15th century there are several literary references linking the diamond to marriages, and it is then that we first find evidence of diamond betrothal or wedding rings. Possibly one of the earliest examples of a betrothal ring with diamonds once belonged to Mary, Duchess of Burgundy in 1477 (fig. 2.20). It was given to her on the occasion of her marriage to the Holy Roman Emperor Maximillian I (1459–1519). Diamonds of varying shapes and cuts form her initial 'M', and on the ring shoulders, there are crowns in relief marking her royal status (fig. 2.21).

Fig. 2.17 ABOVE
Ring with Italian inscription
Italy, 14th century
Gold, ruby
The Griffin Collection, on deposit,
The Metropolitan Museum of Art,
New York (L2015.72.11)

Fig. 2.18 OPPOSITE
Brooch showing a betrothed couple
Burgundy or Flanders, c. 1430–40
Gold, enamel, diamond, ruby, pearls
Kunstkammer, Kunsthistorisches
Museum, Vienna

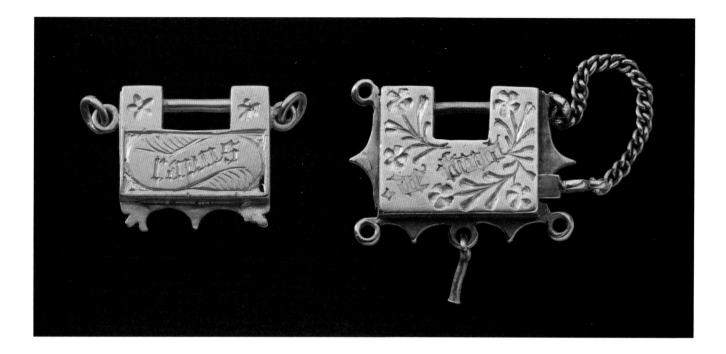

During the 15th century the use and combinations of gemstones proliferated. A gold ring with sapphire and garnet, either French or English from about 1400 (fig. 2.22), is confirmed as a betrothal or love ring by its French inscription: 'oue tout mon coer' (with all my heart). At the time the garnet was probably thought to be a ruby. The diamond became increasingly popular and the cuts more complex, as can be seen in a ring with red enamelled roses and foliage along the hoop and the luxuriant addition of a four-point diamond (fig. 2.23). A 15th-century Italian gold ring features a diamond crystal in its natural octahedral shape which is unusually set sideways, rather than with its point showing upwards, a more common practice at that time (fig. 2.24). More poignant though is its private message revealing the names of the bridal couple: 'Lorenzo a Lena' (from Lorenzo to Lena).

This personalised message naming a loved one anticipates a new era. The Church would start to lose its dominance over everyday life, the wealthy merchant classes would gain influence, artisans would have their own workshops, and portraits would be painted to celebrate individual achievement and status. In jewellery design, the diamond would increasingly be associated with love and marriage.

Fig. 2.20 LEFT
Marriage of Mary, Duchess of Burgundy to the Holy Roman Emperor Maximilian I
from the *Memoirs of Philippe of Commines* (Ms 18f. 185v)
French School, 16th century
Paint on vellum
Musée Dobrée, Nantes

Fig. 2.21 ABOVE
Engagement ring of Mary, Duchess of Burgundy
Flanders, c. 1477
Gold, diamonds
Kunstkammer, Kunsthistorisches Museum, Vienna

Fig. 2.22
Ring with leaf decoration and French inscription
France or England, c. 1400
Gold, garnet, sapphire
Victoria and Albert Museum, London

Fig. 2.23
Ring with four-point diamond
West European, 15th century
Gold, enamel, diamond
The Benjamin Zucker Family Collection

Fig. 2.24
Ring with dedication 'Lorenzo a Lena'
Italy, 15th century
Gold, diamond
British Museum, London

Fig. 3.1
**Portrait of Bianca Maria Sforza
by Ambrogio de Predis**
Milan, Italy, c. 1493
Oil on panel
Widener Collection, National
Gallery of Art, Washington DC

3 From the Renaissance to Baroque
Fidelity and Virtue in Marriage

FROM THE 14TH CENTURY IN ITALY, and well-established Europe-wide by 1500, a revival of interest in the literature and arts of the ancient Greeks and Romans led to a cultural Renaissance. Part of this movement was the rediscovery of classical mythology and poetry. Artists and craftsmen used the great love stories of the Roman poets as sources, such as the *Metamorphoses* by Ovid (43 BC–AD 17/18) and the *Ecologues* by Virgil (70–19 BC), depicting scenes from the stories or incorporating familiar quotations in their works of art. Venus, the Roman goddess of love (known as Aphrodite to the ancient Greeks), and her son Cupid (Eros) featured in paintings, sculpture and jewellery as metaphors for love and desire.

The Italians played a major role in shaping and spreading this taste for classical culture. From the 15th century, the upper classes in Italy were given a humanist education, characterised by the study of classical texts and philosophy, a more critical approach to traditional Christian teaching and, by association, an appreciation for classical art and architecture. Through trade, banking and political alliances, the humanist movement gradually spread to England, France, Germany and the Low Countries (now the Netherlands). By 1550, the Renaissance style was largely established throughout Western Europe, persisting in some countries, such as Spain, well into the 17th century.

Beyond these cultural changes, Europe was experiencing considerable religious and political upheaval. Throughout the 16th century religious protests were fracturing the authority of the Catholic Church. By 1600, many countries had rejected the old church and its customs in favour of reformed Protestant faiths independent from Rome. The Thirty Years War (1618–48) left Europe a divided continent: largely Protestant in the north with a renewed and reformed Catholic church in the south. Inevitably, these religious upheavals influenced everyday customs such as betrothal, marriage and attitudes to morality.

Jewellery played a pivotal role in these customs. In more puritan societies, the wearing of jewels was discouraged for fear of immodesty. More commonly, jewels continued to be on display in the courts and in the noble and wealthy merchant households of Europe. Elaborate jewels depicting love themes in colourful enamels, gemstones and pearls continued to outwardly communicate inner feelings.

Fig. 3.2 ABOVE
Ring
Western Europe, c. 1580-1620
Gold, ruby
Alice and Louis Koch Collection in
the Swiss National Museum, Zurich

Fig. 3.3a and b BELOW
**Gimmel ring with clasped hands
and inscribed marriage vow**
Probably southern Germany,
c. 1570-1600
Gold, diamond, ruby
Alice and Louis Koch Collection in
the Swiss National Museum, Zurich

Fig. 3.4 OPPOSITE
**Portrait of Eleonore of Toledo,
wife of Cosimo I de Medici**
by Agnolo Bronzino
c. 1540
Oil on canvas
Entrance vestibule, Galleria degli
Uffizi, Florence

For the wealthy classes, it became fashionable to have portraits painted to mark the occasion of a wedding and to flaunt the status of the uniting families. The wife would be depicted wearing opulent jewellery, usually her dowry or personal wedding gifts from her husband, as seen in the bridal portrait by Ambrogio de Predis of Bianca Maria Sforza (1472–1510), daughter of Galeazzo Maria Sforza, Duke of Milan (fig. 3.1).

Bianca Maria Sforza became the second spouse of the Holy Roman Emperor Maximilian I (1459–1519), who had given his first wife, Mary of Burgundy, a diamond engagement ring. There is no trace of an engagement ring in Bianca's portrait but, in keeping with the taste of the period, she is shown in profile, a pose echoing ancient Roman portraiture, and in her hair she wears an impressive jewel bearing the motto of the powerful Sforza family, 'MERITO ET TEMPORE' (with merit and time). Among Bianca's sumptuous ornaments is a heavily bejewelled belt studded with large diamonds, rubies and pearls, matched by a pearl necklace with the same pendant gemstones. These were all symbolic of marriage and chastity: the rubies for passionate love, diamonds for virtue and constancy, and pearls for purity. Pearls were also associated with the Virgin Mary (denoting her chastity) and rubies with both Mary and Christ (representing his sacrificial blood), which, together with the carnation flower tucked into her belt, may have been efforts to accentuate Bianca's purity, even though it was her second marriage as well.

To this day, rings are often the most intimate jewels we wear, commemorating a special event in life or carrying personal a message for the wearer. Rubies and diamonds continued to be the primary choice of gemstones for betrothal and wedding rings, either as a single stone ring or two interlocking twin rings, called gimmel rings (figs. 3.2, 3.3a and b), popular in the 16th and 17th centuries.

On one late 16th-century example, a miniature enamelled sculpture of an infant has been concealed inside the bezel, only visible when the two hoops are taken apart.

Fig. 3.5
Ring with clasped right hands
Western Europe, c. 1600-30
Gold, diamonds
Österreichisches Museum für
Angewandte Kunst (MAK), Vienna

On its twin is a skeleton, a reminder of the marriage vow 'until death do us part' as well as a fashionable *memento mori*, a reminder of the inevitability of death and the need to lead a moral life (fig. 3.3b). The two right hands supporting the bezel of the ring are part of the closing mechanism and represent the faith and loyalty expected of the married couple. Often engraved inside the hoops were the marriage vows, either in Latin, as here, 'QUOD DEUS CONNIUNXIT, HOMO NON SEPARAT' (What God has joined, let no man put asunder), or in the vernacular language of their origin, such as English, Netherlandish, German or French.

The *fede* motif of conjoined right hands found on Roman and medieval rings continued in popularity during the Renaissance as a symbol of fidelity and trust. In Italy today, the word *fede* is synonymous with the wedding ring and signifies trust and loyalty. There were numerous variations of this theme but when combined with the diamond, the symbolism became more powerful. (fig. 3.5).

Fig. 3.6
Wedding of Maria de Medici
and Henry IV of France
by Jacopo da Empoli
1600
Oil on canvas
Entrance vestibule, Galleria degli
Uffizi, Florence

The conspicuous message emanating from a portrait of Eleonore of Toledo (1522–62), a young Spanish royal who married into the powerful Medici family in Florence, is that of marriage and high status (fig. 3.4). It was one of many portraits of Eleonore emphasising her exalted status and her renowned style. This portrait by Agnolo Bronzino was painted soon after her marriage to Cosimo I de Medici in 1539. She prominently holds her right hand in front of her, displaying a gold ring with cusped setting and large diamond, and, on her little finger, a ring with a Roman intaglio bearing all the symbols of good luck for marriage: the clasped hands, cornucopia and dove. Ownership of such a ring, which still survives in the Museo degli Argenti in Florence, attests to Eleonore's humanist education and power as Duchess of Florence. The pearls embroidered on her dress and hairnet would have been more than a fashion statement; they also represented chastity. Cosimo even had an emblem designed for Eleonore with a peahen and the motto 'cum pudore laeta fecunditas' (happy fruitfulness with chastity). The marriage was politically successful and the couple produced eleven heirs for the Medici family.

Decades later, in 1600, another member of the Medici family, Marie de Medici (1575–1642) married Henri IV of France (1589–1610). A painting depicts the wedding ceremony in great detail (fig. 3.6). The couple face each other, and Henri places a ring with a pointed diamond on a finger of her right hand, while the Cardinal in the background blesses the union. Diamond rings, featuring either one or multiple diamonds, were much favored in the Renaissance period. The designs not only reflected the imagination of the goldsmith but also indicated the status of the wearer, depending on the size and number of diamonds (figs. 3.7 and 3.8).

In the language of love tokens, the turquoise was considered the stone of friendship, a tradition which was to continue well into the 19th century. An enchanting 16th-century gold ring, with four daisies engraved on the cusps surrounding the central turquoise, conceals a hidden message destined for the recipient of this token of love or friendship (fig. 3.9). The

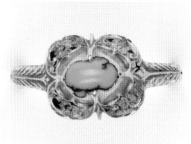

Fig. 3.10 *RIGHT*
Signet ring with winged heart and initials 'FDA'
Probably Germany, 1550–1600
Gold, turquoise
Victoria and Albert Museum,
London

Fig. 3.11 *OPPOSITE*
Signet ring with clasped hands, forget-me-nots, date and initials
Germany, 1634
Gold, *verre eglomisé*
Victoria and Albert Museum,
London

Fig. 3.12
Ring in belt form with French inscription
England or France, 16th century
Gold
Private Collection

daisy was named the flower of love and stood for innocence and modesty. Less subtle is the love message on a signet ring of about 1550 which has an inset turquoise overlaid with an openwork gold silhouette showing a winged heart ornately interlocked with the initials FDA (fig. 3.10).

It is often assumed that larger rings, especially signet rings, were worn by men, as may apply to a German signet ring with a reverse painted crystal seal (fig. 3.11). It depicts an armorial shield bearing the *fede* motif holding three flowers, which appear to be forget-me-nots. An extremely rare commemorative date of 12 June 1634 and the initials AW and GH surround the shield. Was this the date of a betrothal or wedding, or a personal anniversary?

Messages of love were often hidden inside the hoops of rings, their meaning only known to the lovers. A French inscription, 'SVIS A VOUS' (I am yours), inside a ring shaped like a buckled belt is very romantic (fig. 3.12). In many parts of Europe, it was an established tradition to give a bride a marriage belt for her wedding to encourage fertility. In the Cathedral of Prato in Italy, the Holy Girdle of the Virgin Mary has long been venerated as a relic and has become a place of pilgrimage for expectant mothers.

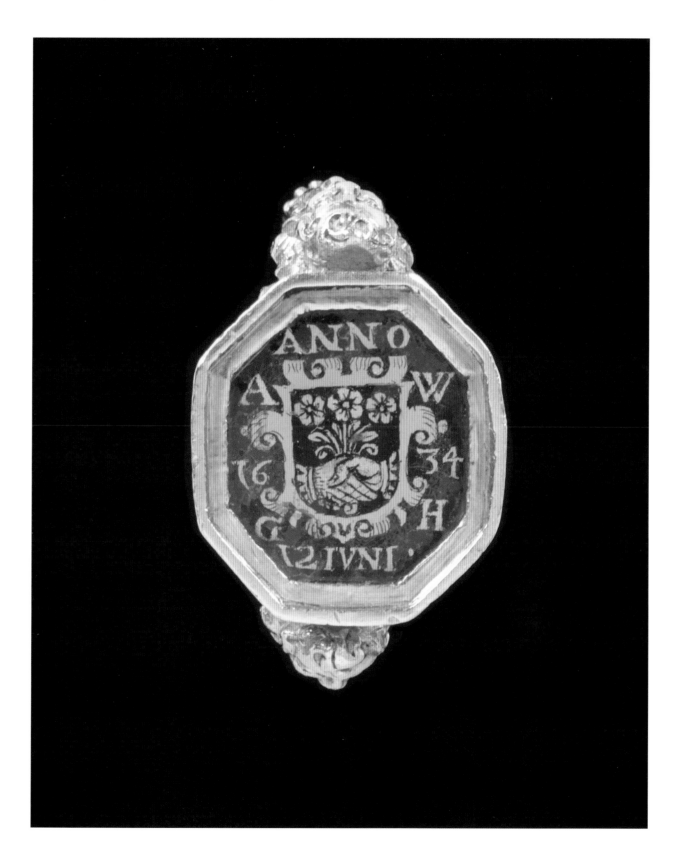

Fig. 3.13
Venus of Urbino by Titian
Completed by 1538
Oil on canvas
Galleria degli Uffizi, Florence

Fig. 3.14
Ring with dog
Latin inscription 'I shall be faithful
unto death'
Italy, c. 1540–60
Gold, enamel
Alice and Louis Koch Collection in
the Swiss National Museum, Zurich

Fig. 3.15 *BELOW LEFT*
**Ring with heart, female figure
and unicorn**
Southern Germany, c. 1550–1600
Gold, enamel, diamond
Rijksmuseum, Amsterdam

Fig. 3.16 *BELOW RIGHT*
Salamander pendant
Gold, diamonds, pearls, enamel
16th century
Museo degli Argenti, Florence

The depiction of love and marriage in Renaissance paintings was often cryptic and deciphering it relied on a humanist education. Venus, the Roman goddess of love, featured prominently. In the *Venus of Urbino* painted by Titian in 1534, she is depicted as a classical nude lying erotically on her bed and surrounded by nuptial symbols (fig. 3.13). Here, Venus is a metaphor for the bride-to-be: she holds roses in her hand, which she will be wearing at her ceremony. On the window sill stands a myrtle bush in a pot, a symbol for beauty, youth and love. In the background are two richly decorated *cassoni* (wedding chests) which stored precious objects, and two maidens are preparing her bridal outfit, one of them with the bridal dress slung over her shoulder. Curled up at the foot of her bed is a small dog, traditionally associated with loyalty. Pendants with Venus figures were popular during the Renaissance, as were rings with miniature dog sculptures conveying messages of love and loyalty. Some of these rings even included inscriptions inside the hoop referring to faithfulness beyond death (fig. 3.14).

Other animals could also serve as metaphors for love. A sculptural ring of the second half of the 16th century boasts a wealth of love emblems: a central red enamelled heart crowned by a diamond is flanked by a female figure draped in blue supporting the heart with her right hand, with a crouching unicorn holding it up with his horn (fig. 3.15). The lower part of the ring, unseen when worn, is the *fede* motif. The unicorn is shown here as a white horse with a twisted horn. According to mythology, this beast could only be tamed by a virgin maiden, which led to its association with chaste love and fidelity in marriage. In a Christian context, the story became an allegory for the Virgin Mary. Although the unicorn is often depicted on paintings and tapestries, it is rare on a ring. What might the giver's message mean? Did he express a wish to be tamed by his lover?

Jewels with a salamander, an amphibious lizard-like creature, were fashionable love tokens, and given by both men and women (fig. 3.16). In the classical world,

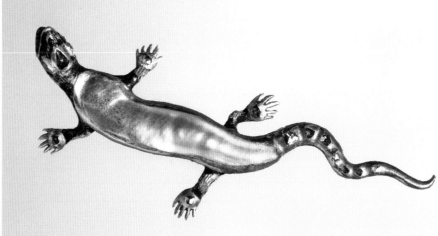

the supposed ability of the salamander to survive or even extinguish fire was shrouded in mystery. The myth may have arisen from the habit of these creatures to hibernate in undergrowth but emerge from kindling when taken indoors for lighting fires. When a salamander jewel was worn, it signified passionate or ardent love. A gold salamander pendant jewel set with rubies was found in the wreck of the *Girona*, a ship from the England-bound Spanish Armada which sank in the Irish Sea in 1588. It probably belonged to a seaman on board who never returned home.

The association between music and love can be found throughout art and literature since ancient times. The Assyrian goddess of love, Ishtar, played the lute and its sensuous tones would evoke harmony and the pleasures of love. In Greek mythology, Terpsichore, the muse of lyric poetry and dance, would play the lyre. In ancient Egypt, the sound of the harp would bring happiness. During the 16th and 17th centuries, the symbolism of music would have been familiar to a European humanist audience and numerous paintings and prints of the period show lovers playing musical instruments. Music has the ability of expressing emotions; men and women sing about being in love, love lost, and the feelings that accompany love. Jewels depicting musical instruments belonged to the language of love and romance. A Renaissance pendant shaped like a lute, from about 1600, was a coded message to a loved one (fig. 3.17). The combination of rubies for passionate love, white enamelled daisies for innocence, pearls for chastity and emeralds for love and hope, all spoke of romance.

Love was a common theme in the theatre of the 16th and 17th centuries. The *innamorati* (the Lovers) were stock characters from the Italian tradition of popular

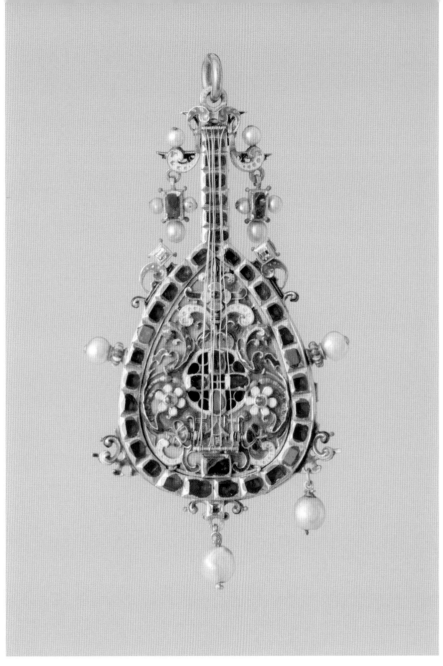

Fig. 3.17
Pendant in the form of a lute
Germany, c. 1600
Gold, enamel, emeralds, rubies, diamonds, pearls
Rijksmuseum, Amsterdam

Fig. 3.18 RIGHT
Pendant with *Commedia dell'arte* characters by Giovanni Battista Scolari
1568
Gold, enamel, baroque pearl, emeralds, diamonds, rubies
Museo degli Argenti, Florence

Fig. 3.19 OPPOSITE
Allegory of the Triumph of Venus with Cupid, Folly and Time **by Agnolo Bronzino**
c. 1545
Oil on wood
National Gallery, London

comedy called *Commedia dell'arte*. Played like a comedy of errors, the Lovers had to overcome a series of impediments before they were finally united. Also known as the *Comédie Italienne* in France, this theatrical tradition continued into the 18th century. The stories captured the imagination of Renaissance goldsmiths who fashioned jewels depicting the characters. On one pendant of 1568, the Lovers are seated in a gondola shaped from a baroque pearl, surrounded by rubies, emeralds, enamelled forget-me-nots and suspended pearls (fig. 3.18).

The most commonly depicted character in art and jewellery associated with love is Cupid, the son of the goddess Venus. In an allegorical painting of about 1545 by the Florentine artist Agnolo Bronzino, Venus is embraced by Cupid, who lovingly kisses her (fig. 3.19). Venus clutches a golden apple with her left hand and in her right is Cupid's arrow, the emblem of desire. The billing doves at bottom left represent romance. Above Venus the personification of Time with his hourglass tries to snatch the arrow, while the *putto* (cherub) playing with roses represents folly and pleasure. The howling figure on the left may represent the jealousy and despair that can accompany love. Cupid wears on his belt a large ruby and Venus a crown set with pearls and emeralds alluding to love and desire. The painter was known to be a keen poet and was inspired by the erotic love sonnets of Francesco Petrarca (1304–74). The central theme of the poet's *Il Canzoniere* is his love of Laura, a theme later echoed in William Shakespeare's play *Romeo and Juliet*.

The symbolism of love found in poetry and paintings would have been known to contemporary goldsmiths and undoubtedly sparked their creativity when creating gifts for lovers to exchange. Cupid was most commonly depicted on pendants and lockets, from magnificently jewelled gold pieces to more modest examples. An ornate pendant embellished with gemstones from about 1600 shows Cupid as the god of desire, attraction and affection, in white enamel with an arrow (his attribute) in gold. It employs all the stones associated with love: diamonds, rubies, pearls and emeralds. Adding to the romantic theme are a pair of billing doves (fig. 3.20). Symbolically, the person struck by Cupid's arrow falls in love, possibly the intended message for the recipient of this jewel. The same sentiment applies to more modest love tokens. An English silver locket of 1690–1700 features an embossed image of Cupid drawing his bowstring to release the arrow and is surrounded by the inscription 'NOE HEART MORE TRVE THEN MINE TO YOV' (fig. 3.21). Similar locket pendants were produced to celebrate the marriage of Charles II to Catherine of Braganza in 1662.

In 16th- and 17th-century imagery, the heart continued to be associated with romantic love. A small ring of around 1620–50 with a crowned heart-shaped sapphire clasped by two hands in loyalty (fig. 3.22) was clearly a gift of love. When the bezel is opened, the Roman numerals XX are revealed, perhaps a personal message from a loved one, a significant number in a relationship or commemorating a wedding anniversary. The choice of a sapphire, the gemstone of emotion and romantic love, would have been intentional.

In a jewel commissioned as a wedding gift around 1600, a red enamelled heart forms the central motif (fig. 3.23). The heart is set with a diamond and held by two hands with diamond studded cuffs as a sign of fidelity.

Fig. 3.20 OPPOSITE
Pendant with Cupid and billing doves
Germany, c. 1600
Gold, enamel, pearls, emeralds, rubies
Rijksmuseum, Amsterdam

Fig. 3.21
Locket with Cupid and love inscription
England, 1690–1700
Silver
Victoria and Albert Museum, London

Fig. 3.22
Ring with heart-shaped sapphire
Western Europe, c. 1620–50
Gold, enamel, sapphire
Alice and Louis Koch Collection in the Swiss National Museum, Zurich

Prominently positioned below is a large diamond in a box setting. These gemstones, in combination with additional amatory devices such as nuzzling doves, cornucopiae, parrots for abundance and a phoenix wishing for new life, all convey the very best wishes for a long, happy and virtuous marriage blessed with many children.

A portrait of Lady Anne Carleton (1585?–1627), of about 1625, shows her wearing a bodice jewel attached to a red bow with a heart-shaped gemstone in the centre (fig. 3.24). It appears to be a large sapphire or diamond framed by smaller diamonds, although it is often difficult to identify gemstones in paintings. She wears pearls in her hair and pinned to her dress is a locket, which may have concealed a miniature portrait of her husband Dudley Carleton, 1st Viscount Dorchester, who was a diplomat, art collector and Secretary of State under Charles I of England. Unlike this ostentatious display of jewels, probably included to demonstrate Lady Carleton's marital status, his accompanying portraits are more austere.

Fig. 3.23 OPPOSITE
Marriage pendant with symbols of love
Southern Germany, c. 1580-1600
Gold, enamel, pearls, diamonds
Rijksmuseum, Amsterdam

Fig. 3.24 ABOVE
Portrait of Anne, Lady Carleton wearing heart-shaped pendant by studio of Michiel Jansz. van Miereveldt
c. 1625
National Portrait Gallery, London

Fig. 3.25a and b
The Gresley Jewel
Miniatures by Nicholas Hilliard
England, c. 1574
Gold, enamel, rubies, pearls
Victoria and Albert Museum,
London

In the 16th and 17th centuries, miniature portraits concealed in beautiful bejewelled lockets became increasingly fashionable, either presented as diplomatic gifts or exchanged between lovers and married couples. The Gresley Jewel is an exquisitely enamelled locket decorated with pearls and small figures of Cupid shooting an arrow (figs. 3.25a and b), which opens to reveal miniatures of Sir Thomas Gresley (1552–1610) and his wife Catherine Walsingham (c. 1568–1637). They were painted by the highly regarded artist and miniaturist Nicholas Hilliard, who was also trained as a goldsmith and undertook commissions from Queen Elizabeth I. When the locket is closed, they face each other.

A ruby and diamond locket, probably made by a jeweller at the Imperial Court workshops of Prague around 1610–20, has a secret compartment on the reverse containing a miniature portrait of a man (fig. 3.26). When worn it was hidden to the viewer but close to the heart of the wearer. The front bears a heart-shaped ruby pierced by an arrow and is surrounded by rubies and diamonds. The message of the jewelled locket could not be more explicit.

Dress fashions and styles in jewellery were increasingly led by France in the 17th century, a period and style later termed 'Baroque' after various European words for an irregular pearl, such as the Italian *barocco*. The term characterises the ornate exuberance and vivacity experienced in the architecture, sculpture and painting of the period. The world and its riches were being opened up to explorers, and botanical surveys were becoming more common. This interest in botany resulted in a fashion for flowers and plants across the visual arts and a language of flowers developed in jewellery. Richly enamelled lockets were ideal canvases for naturalistic flower compositions and their metaphorical significance. Enamelled on the back of a northern European gold locket of about 1680 is a closed red and white tulip with yellow tinges, flanked by a rose and a sunflower (figs. 3.27a and b). On the front, the tulip is wide open with three diamonds crowning the scene. The tulip was introduced to Europe from Persia where it was a symbol of true love. In the language of flowers, the sunflower stood for devotion or dedicated love and the rose, the flower of Venus, for romantic love.

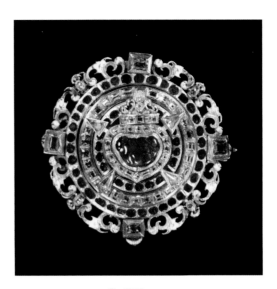

Fig. 3.26
Locket with concealed miniature of a loved one
Prague, c. 1610–20
Gold, enamel, rubies, diamonds, oil on metal
Victoria and Albert Museum, London

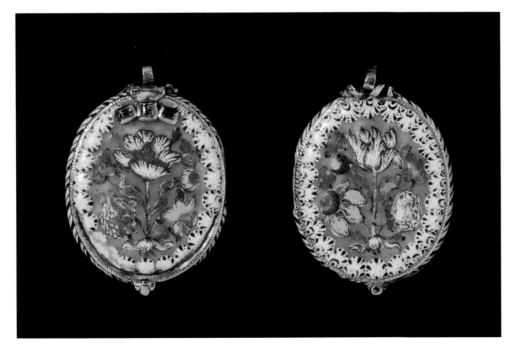

Fig. 3.27a and b
Locket with tulip, rose, daffodil and sunflower
Northern Europe, c. 1680
Gold, enamel, diamonds
Victoria and Albert Museum, London

As the 17th century progressed, women's fashions changed from dark velvets and brocades to dresses made of silks and satins in pastel shades. Against the backdrop of these luminous fabrics, sensuous pearls were favoured, chiefly in chokers worn tightly around the neck and as drop pearl earrings. During the long reign of Louis XIV of France (1638–1715), a number of influential mistresses at court were painted wearing the new fashions in jewellery. It was rumored that Louise Elisabeth Rouxel, also known as Madame de Grancy (1653–1711), had a brief liaison with the Sun King himself. She remained unmarried and was revered for her beauty. In a portrait painted by Claude Lefèbvre around 1665, she is depicted in a white dress with red cloak held to her breast, accompanied by a mischievous Cupid aiming his arrow at her (fig. 3.28). She wears highly fashionable pearls, and on her arms and over her sleeves she wears bracelets made of gold with rubies and diamonds. Both the subject matter and the jewels, and the roses in the background and in her hair, suggest a story of romance and love, rather than of marriage. In portraits of the second half of the 17th century, wealthy women wear pearls in abundance, although many of these original pieces have not survived. Pearls are naturally grown from living organisms and are delicate and thus prone to perish over time.

It was also fashionable to wear diamonds in combination with pearls. Diamonds were considered indestructible, revered for their extreme hardness. They became the ideal gift from the bridegroom to his bride, as they symbolised fortitude and constancy. From the evidence of contemporary accounts, it was now customary for the bride to receive a valuable diamond ring on the occasion of her betrothal as well as a plain gold wedding band at her wedding. Diamond rings rarely had a single large stone; it was more common to wear them in clusters (figs. 3.29 and 3.30). Increasingly, however, yellow gold settings were regarded as old fashioned. Newly explored techniques for cutting diamonds led to complex rose and brilliant cuts creating ever more refractions of light and sparkle. When set in silver, the whiteness of the diamond was enhanced.

Fig. 3.28 OPPOSITE
Portrait of Louise Elisabeth Rouxel, known as Madame de Grancy, by Claude Lefèbvre
c. 1665
Oil on canvas
Château de Versailles

Fig. 3.29 RIGHT
Cluster ring
Netherlands, 1670–90
Gold, enamel, rose-cut diamonds
Rijksmuseum, Amsterdam

Fig. 3.30 FAR RIGHT
Ring with seven diamonds
Western Europe, late 17th century
Gold, table-cut diamonds
The Benjamin Zucker Family
Collection

MADEMOISELLE
DE·KEROUALLE
ENSVITE
DUCHESSE·DE
PORTSMOUTH
ET·D'AUBIGNY·

A magnificent bodice jewel/pendant from about 1700 boasts diamonds in varying colours and complex rose-cuts, with a large pear-shaped briolette-cut diamond at the bottom set in silver to maximise the sparkle (fig. 3.32). It would not only have demonstrated wealth and status, but also, one would hope, of great love and affection. Louise de Kérouaille (1649–1734), Duchess of Portsmouth and the mistress of Charles II, is wearing such a diamond jewel on her low-cut dress (fig. 3.31). The shell she holds in her hands, overflowing with pearls and a coral branch (an amulet for children), suggests fertility and is symbolic of the son she bore from this liaison.

At his deathbed, Charles voiced concerns that, as well as the queen, both his mistresses the Duchess of Portsmouth and Nell Gwynn (1650–87), should be supported after his death. A diamond jewel inscribed on the reverse, 'The gift of Charles 2nd to Nell Gwynne', was handed down through the family from Charles Beauclerk, 1st Duke of St Albans, the illegitimate son of Nell Gwynn by the king. The relic of this famous love story was much treasured and was adapted in its later life, the constant diamond still surviving, albeit as a hatpin (fig. 3.33).

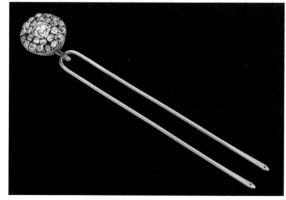

4 The Eighteenth Century
Exuberant Expressions of Love

WITH THE DEATH OF LOUIS XIV of France in 1715, court etiquette and highly prescribed social customs such as betrothal and marriage were relaxed. Across Europe formal wedding ceremonies and witnesses were no longer essential, and there was greater flexibility in arranging marriage contracts. Men could promise marriage at a future date, and if they had consummated their relationship beforehand it then became a legally binding agreement. The traditional religious wedding ceremony was being questioned and in some instances even rejected. However, the social and moral codes of chastity and fidelity, duty and justice were values that were expected from the couple. For the most part, the aristocracy continued the tradition of arranged marriages, for gaining wealth and property and making political alliances, but the abundance of sentimental jewellery produced during the 18th century attests to the desire for love and romance across the social classes.

During the first half of the 18th century, France was the arbiter of taste and etiquette throughout Europe. For high society, it was a period of unlicensed freedom, which found expression in the idyllic paintings of the period showing flirtatious scenes known as *fêtes galantes*. These were pastoral scenes of men and women engaged in romantic play or of lovers serenading young women, such as *The Music Lesson* by François Boucher (fig. 4.1). Inspired by such paintings, goldsmiths made elaborate lockets and pocket watches decorated with enamelled amorous scenes often framed by the symbols of love, such as billing doves, flowers and a trumpet-wielding Cupid (fig. 4.2).

From the 1730s, the visual arts were inspired by the playful style of the French Court, now known as the Louis XV or Rococo style. As with architecture, painting and other decorative arts, jewellery designs were naturalistic and highly ornamental with sinuous curves, asymmetry and a flamboyant use of flowers, leaves, birds and shells. Except for mourning jewellery, the spirit of designs was joyous and lighthearted and jewellers showed a distinct preference for pretty pastel shades of enamel, and gemstones in a bright array of colours, sometimes with underlying foils to intensify the effect. Contemporary interest in nature and its beauty resulted in a rich, florid style, with floral-shaped settings for stones and swirling foliage.

The Rococo style remained in fashion until the 1760s, by when a new taste began to establish itself in the courts of Europe. Neoclassicism reflected a revival of interest

Fig. 4.1
The Music Lesson
by François Boucher
1749
Oil on canvas
Musée Cognacq-Jay, Paris

Fig. 4.2 OPPOSITE
**Watch with amorous scene,
movement by Julien le Roy**
France or Switzerland, 1750-60
Vari-coloured gold, enamel
Victoria and Albert Museum,
London

Fig. 4.3 ABOVE
**Wedding ring crowned heart
and dated inscription**
England, 1706
Gold, silver, diamonds
Victoria and Albert Museum,
London

Fig. 4.4 BELOW, LEFT
Heart pendant
Flanders, c. 1785–1800
Silver, diamonds
Rijksmuseum, Amsterdam

Fig. 4.5 BELOW, RIGHT
Bow-shaped brooch
Netherlands, 1784
Gold, silver, diamonds
Rijksmuseum, Amsterdam

in classical art and architecture caused by recent archaeological discoveries made in Italy. Influenced by treasures uncovered at Herculaneum in 1713 and at Pompeii in 1755, goldsmiths once again adopted the formal symmetry of ancient classical design. Compositions were lightened by festoons, tassels and swags, and sentimental themes were still highly popular in jewellery, developing into increasingly elaborate designs towards the end of the century.

Diamonds dominated jewellery in the 18th century. This was made possible after 1725 when the Portuguese discovered new diamond mines in Brazil. European royalty and aristocracy were festooned with diamonds. Marie-Antoinette, Queen of France (1755–93), Catherine the Great, Empress of Russia (1729–96), Maria Theresa, Empress of the Holy Roman Empire (1717–80) and Queen Charlotte of England (1744–1818) were style icons of their day and wore copious quantities of diamonds. Increasingly intricate diamond cuts were introduced, and underlying foils and silver settings enhanced the whiteness of the stones which sparkled in the evening candlelight.

Diamonds became desirable expressions of love and marriage. Goldsmiths fashioned exuberant floral sprays and garlands, often favouring asymmetrical compositions. The heart remained the most popular symbol of love, as seen in a marriage ring with a dated inscription, 'Dudley & Katherine united 26th March 1706'. It consists of a heart-shaped diamond, crowned and supported by hands of loyalty (fig. 4.3). This fashionable composition resembled the Flemish heart, a design which originated in Catholic Flanders, a region whose culture was steeped in religious devotion. Here, crowned heart pendants were originally given on the day celebrating mothers and the Virgin Mary. The device was soon found in diamond-studded love tokens (fig. 4.4), sometimes displayed alongside other emblems such as the trophy of love (an arrangement of love symbols including a torch), or a quiver and bow symbolising Cupid (also known as Amor).

Jewelled bows studded with colourful gemstones, pearls and diamonds were highly fashionable in the latter part of the 17th century and continued to be worn as bodice ornaments well into the next. The designs imitated textile bows and were highly intricate but were not, as may first appear, simply decorative accessories. They have been associated with the true lover's knot, a symbol of love and affection or everlasting love (fig. 4.5). The diamond example shown here was adapted by the goldsmith Adrianus Steen in 1784. He removed it from a church monstrance and transformed it into a brooch to become a love token. Jewels were handed down from one generation to the next and adapted in design or size. In this case it had even changed function.

Rings continued to be given in betrothal or during a wedding ceremony, as depicted in Joseph Highmore's (1692–1780) painting of the marriage scene of Pamela and Mr. B (fig. 4.6) from the hugely popular novel *Pamela; or Virtue Rewarded* by Samuel Richardson (1689–1761). Pamela Andrews is a fifteen-year old maid-servant whose master, a country landowner, continually tries to seduce her before finally doing the honourable thing and marrying her.

The diamond maintained its significance as a gemstone associated with marriage, continuing to symbolise virtue and constancy in the marriage union. The most affordable form of diamond ring was one with smaller gemstones set in clusters, rather than one larger single stone. Some were adapted to resemble a flower, such as a daisy or marguerite, both flowers associated with love (fig. 4.8). Clusters might consist solely of diamonds, or diamonds combined with rubies, their deep red colour representing passionate love and Venus, the goddess of love (fig. 4.7). Gemstones set in heart shapes were a common design for marriage rings, often surmounted by a crown, which denoted loyalty (fig. 4.9).

Rings for betrothals, weddings or other declarations of love sometimes included emeralds, associated with hope, love and chastity. The combination of stones could signify a variety of meanings, some of which may remain unknown. A ruby and diamond ring surrounded by a wreath of small emeralds could be interpreted as everlasting love, with the wreath mimicking myrtle or rosemary, plants both associated with weddings (fig. 4.10).

Some brides preferred the simple gold band, especially in England. These were called posy rings after the verses or *poesies* inscribed on them, which were mainly hidden inside the hoop and so only known to the giver and recipient.

Goldsmiths found great inspiration in the mythologies and symbolism of love, which were familiar to their educated clients. Love could be represented as a delicate butterfly set in diamonds and worn as a ring (fig. 4.11). The significance of the butterfly goes back to classical mythology and to Psyche, the wife of Cupid. The beautiful princess Psyche was so greatly admired by men that Venus felt neglected. She instructed her son Cupid to make Psyche fall in love with a monster, but the plan

Fig. 4.7 ABOVE, LEFT
Four cluster rings
Western Europe, 18th century
Gold, silver, rubies, diamonds
Musée du Louvre, Paris

Fig. 4.8 ABOVE
Cluster Ring shaped like a flower
Probably England, c. 1750-80
Gold, silver, diamonds
Rijksmuseum, Amsterdam

Fig. 4.9
Ring with crowned heart
Probably Spain, c. 1760
Gold, silver, emerald, ruby, diamond
Alice and Louis Koch Collection in
the Swiss National Museum, Zurich

Fig. 4.10
Love ring
Western Europe, 1730-60
Gold, silver, diamonds, emeralds,
rubies
Victoria and Albert Museum,
London

Fig. 4.11
Ring with butterfly
Western Europe, 18th century
Gold, diamonds
Private Collection

Fig. 4.12
Ring with ape-headed Cupid holding a heart-shaped mirror
Probably England, c. 1750-60
Gold, silver, enamel, rubies, diamonds
Alice and Louis Koch Collection in the Swiss National Museum, Zurich

Fig. 4.13
Ring with Cupid clasping a flaming heart
England, 1725
Gold, enamel, ruby
Victoria and Albert Museum, London

Fig. 4.14a and b
Swivel ring with Cupid reaching for a heart and portrait of a young woman
Switzerland, c. 1730
Gold, enamel
Alice and Louis Koch Collection in the Swiss National Museum, Zurich

rebounded when they fell in love. Venus consented to her son's marriage and granted Psyche immortality. She is often represented as a butterfly as a symbol of eternity and perpetual love.

Cupid appears in many guises throughout the 18th century. One ring shows Cupid with an ape's head, denoting lust, excess or debauchery, looking into a mirror made of a heart-shaped ruby, a metaphor for vanity (fig. 4.12). The ape/Cupid is surrounded by foliage and roses set with rubies and diamonds. The love theme is confirmed by the French inscription along the outer side of the hoop, 'A VOUS SANS PARTAGE' (for you undivided).

A charming ring with humorous undertones features a miniature enamelled sculpture of Cupid absconding with a flaming heart set with a ruby (fig. 4.13). Along the hoop is an English inscription, 'STOP THIEF'. Cupid is frequently depicted across the arts as a *putto*, plural *putti*, a term which derives from the Italian for a boy or child, usually a plump male child, naked and winged. These cherubic infants were also known as *amorini*. François Boucher's painting *Cupid's Target* (1758) was based on the mid-18th-century ballet *Les Amours des Dieux* and shows playful winged *putti/amorini* holding a target with a heart (fig. 4.15). They are surrounded by all the traditional symbols of love and marriage: a bridal wreath, nuzzling doves, bows and arrows and rose garlands.

A love token of 1730, in the form of an enamelled swivel ring, shows Cupid/Amor with his bow and arrow, reaching for a red heart in a thorny bush (fig. 4.14b). The scene is taken from a book of emblems by Otthonis Vaeni (1609) which features a version of the French inscription found on the ring, 'après la peine le plaisir' (after the pain comes pleasure). Such emblems were inspirational sources for goldsmiths. The other side of the bezel shows a portrait of a young woman, suggesting the ring was worn by her lover (fig. 4.14a). With the swivel mechanism he could turn the bezel, thereby concealing the identity of the woman of his heart.

Many portraits of the period show a wife or mistress wearing a bracelet featuring a miniature of their loved one. In a portrait of about 1760 by François Boucher, Madame de Pompadour (1721–64) wears a highly fashionable multi-stranded pearl bracelet prominently displaying a cameo of Louis XV of France (1710–74) in an

Fig. 4.15
Cupid's Target
by François Boucher
1758
Oil on canvas
Musée du Louvre, Paris

Fig. 4.16
Portrait of Jeanne-Antoinette Poisson, Marquise de Pompadour by François Boucher
1758
Oil on canvas
Fogg Museum, Harvard University, Cambridge, Massachusetts

Fig. 4.17
Queen Charlotte's wedding ring with portrait of George III
1761
Gold, diamonds, miniature on ivory
The Royal Collection of Her Majesty Queen Elizabeth II

Fig. 4.18
Queen Charlotte's keeper ring
1761
Gold, diamonds, sapphire
The Royal Collection of Her Majesty Queen Elizabeth II

Fig. 4.19
Ring with blackamoor and French inscription
England, c. 1765
Gold, enamel, diamonds
Alice and Louis Koch Collection in the Swiss National Museum, Zurich

emerald and diamond setting (fig. 4.16). As his official chief mistress, she wielded great political power and influence over the king and was a patron of the arts.

Miniature portraits set in a jewel with a head or half figure of the bride or bridegroom commemorated a forthcoming union, and were presented or exchanged as wedding jewels. On 8 September 1761, King George III of England gave his wife Queen Charlotte a suite of diamond and pearl jewels to mark the day of their wedding. The set included a gold ring with diamonds and a miniature on ivory with the king's portrait (fig. 4.17).

Charlotte Papendiek (1765–1839), who was assistant keeper and reader to her Majesty, wrote about the queen's court and private life. She mentioned the ring and that it was to be worn on the little finger of the right hand on their wedding day. She lists the full set of jewels and comments that these personal gifts were in addition to the magnificent jewellery formerly in the collection of George II, so that the queen's jewel collection could now not be rivalled by those of Continental royalty. Included in the wedding suite was a ring studded with diamonds along the full circle of the hoop. According to Papendiek's account, the diamonds were not to stand higher than the wedding ring. Instead it was intended to act as a guard to it and was therefore described as a keeper's ring (fig. 4.18).

An unusual theme is explored in an English ring of about 1765, showing a finely enamelled kneeling figure of a black African wearing a turban, with red enamelled floral sprigs and diamonds on either side (fig. 4.19). The figure, then known as a 'blackamoor', would be a metaphor for enslaved love and the French inscription on the hoop reads 'JADORE SE QUI ME BRÛLE' (I adore/love the one who enflames me), a passionate declaration of love.

Masquerade balls were highly fashionable events. The city of Venice, with its long tradition of carnival festivities dating back to the 11th century, was famous for its theatrical costumes and traditions. Entertainingly described by the adventurer

Fig. 4.20a and b
Masquerade ring with forget-me-nots
Western Europe, c. 1760
Gold, enamel, diamonds
Private Collection

Fig. 4.21 OVERLEAF
The Progress of Love: The Lover Crown'd **by Jean-Honoré Fragonard**
1771
Oil on canvas
The Frick Collection, New York

Giacomo Casanova (1725–98) in his salacious memoirs, Venetian carnivals in the mid-18th century were riotous affairs and morals were loose. Veils and black velvet masks led to flirtatious encounters and offered the wearer the advantage of anonymity. Goldsmiths in Italy, France and England developed jewellery with the masked woman as a symbol of love (figs. 4.20a and b). In a ring showing a masked face, the message in French, 'Je cache mes amours' (I mask my love), is concealed on the underside of the bezel, known only to the wearer. The forget-me-not flowers on the ring shoulder add to the romance.

At the French court, a popular form of entertainment was open-air parties held in gardens and private parks featuring follies, pavilions or temples. These *fêtes champêtres* (pastoral feasts) encouraged playful and amorous encounters. Madame du Barry (1743–93), the last of the many official mistresses of Louis XV of France, commissioned the painter Jean Honoré Fragonard to paint four canvases for her pavilion at Château de Louveciennes with the theme *The Progress of Love*. The scenes were entitled 'The Pursuit', 'The Meeting', 'The Love Letter' and 'The Lover Crown'd' (fig. 4.21). In a lush and overgrown garden, with rose bushes and orange trees in large pots and a statue of a sleeping Cupid in the background, is a woman seated on a plinth. She holds a crown over a young man kneeling in front of her with his hands on her lap. He looks adoringly at her, while she turns her head towards the artist on the right sketching the scene. The crowning is reminiscent of the wreath or bridal crown symbolising maidenhood, and the gesture of the woman seems to suggest commitment to marriage and an underlying eroticism.

Such *fête champêtre* scenes were miniaturised in jewels, chiefly on brooches and rings, and given as tokens of love. Two Austrian rings from about 1790, with gold foiled silhouettes against green or bright blue backdrops, belong to this genre. One shows a tree with a man climbing up a ladder to reach a heart at its top (fig. 4.22), with the French inscription 'Incité par Amour' (inspired by love). The other depicts two altars of love with flaming hearts (fig. 4.23), linked by garlands forming an arch and held by two doves in flight. The French inscription 'Nous sommes unis' (We are united in love) underlines the imagery.

Fig. 4.22
Ring with man reaching for a heart in a tree
Probably Austria, c. 1790
Gold, silver, glass, glass paste, foil
Alice and Louis Koch Collection in the Swiss National Museum, Zurich

Fig. 4.23
Ring with flaming hearts on altars of love
Probably Austria, c. 1790
Gold, glass, foil
Alice and Louis Koch Collection in the Swiss National Museum, Zurich

The altar of love was a popular emblem, often situated in a landscaped garden. On a German ring of about 1800 (fig. 4.24), two entwined and flaming hearts rest on an altar with the declaration 'Unsere Verbindung macht uns glücklich' (Our relationship makes us happy). The ring bezel is surrounded by seed pearls, symbolising chastity or perhaps innocence. Like today, people kept locks of hair in a treasured place. Goldsmiths would artistically integrate the hair into decorative scenes or inscriptions, as seen in fig. 4.24 and on another ring depicting an altar of love with two billing doves (fig. 4.25). Above them is the French inscription 'L'AMOUR' (love), the whole scene framed by pearls. It is often impossible to confirm if rings featuring an altar of love were given as love tokens or as wedding rings. However, a ring with a diamond-studded bezel showing the initials JMC on the front, surrounded by a laurel wreath, was clearly made for a married recipient. When opened, a miniature scene with an altar of love is revealed on the reverse of this panel, with the initials MJC on the opposite side, the last initial denoting the same surname (figs. 4.26a and b).

All of the scenes were made from hair. The front panel swivels so that the wearer can choose to have the initials facing each other inside the ring. Above the altar is the French declaration of love 'AMOUR NOUS A UNIS' (Love has united us), which confirms their union. Mourning rings of a similar design but depicting urns and grieving figures were also made using hair, to express love after death.

Other themes which appear to be merely decorative have meanings that are now unfamiliar to us but would have been understood in the 18th century as part of the unwritten language of love. Paintings and prints showing a girl releasing a dove from a birdcage would have alluded to a girls' virginity. This theme is found

Fig. 4.24
Ring with altar of love and flaming heart
Germany, c. 1770–1800
Rose gold, miniature on ivory, hair, seed pearls
Alice and Louis Koch Collection in the Swiss National Museum, Zurich

Fig. 4.25
Brooch with billing doves on an altar of love
England or France, c. 1775–1800
Gold, seed pearls
Victoria and Albert Museum, London

Fig. 4.26a and b
Ring with initials and concealed symbols of love
Germany, c. 1800
Gold, silver, diamonds, bone, hair
Alice and Louis Koch Collection in the Swiss National Museum, Zurich

on a ring based on a print titled *Friendship* by the Swiss artist Angelika Kaufmann (1741–1807), who settled in England. The pearls framing the picture emphasise the innocence of the young girl (fig. 4.27).

Riddles and rebuses (puzzles using pictures and letters to spell out words and phrases) were all the rage in the late 18th century and were ideal for hiding and playing with declarations of love on jewels. The intricate rings of the 1780s and 1790s featuring large bezels provided fitting backdrops. A ring, probably English, displaying a maritime scene at dusk, shows two galleons at sea and a man and woman on the shore in the foreground (fig. 4.28). Possibly a riddle, the scene could be interpreted to mean 'Friend-ship' with the initials JBG on the white flag as those of the loved one. A rebus can be seen on a French blue enamelled ring displaying in gold letters: 'L fait mes d' followed by lily flowers (fig. 4.29). As the French for a stylised lily was 'fleur-de-lis', this rebus can be deciphered as 'Elle fait mes delices' (She makes me happy).

In England, eye portraits known as Lover's Eyes are thought to have originated from a love affair shrouded in secrecy. The Prince of Wales, the future George IV (1762–1830) became infatuated with a widow, Mrs Maria Fitzherbert (1756–1836), when both were visiting the opera in 1784 (fig. 4.30). He proposed she should become his mistress, but, being Catholic, this was unacceptable to her. The prince threatened to kill himself if she would not marry him and pursued her until she consented. Georgiana, the Duchess of Devonshire, who accompanied Maria to the prince's residence, gave her one of her own rings to formalise the marriage. In 1785 George sent Mrs Fitzherbert a written marriage proposal and, instead of a ring, a portrait of his right eye painted by the miniaturist Richard Cosway. They had

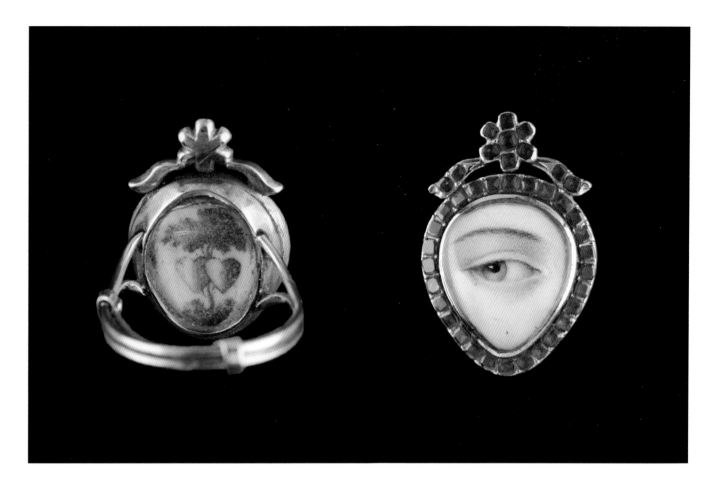

Fig. 4.31 ABOVE
Heart-shaped ring with Lover's Eye
England, c. 1790
Gold, hessonite garnet, ivory
The Skier Collection of Eye
Miniatures, USA

Fig. 4.32 OPPOSITE
**Brooch with Lover's Eye
surrounded by clouds**
England, c. 1800
Silver, gold, diamonds
The Skier Collection of Eye
Miniatures, USA

a clandestine wedding ceremony and he received a portrait of her eye in return. As the union was never approved by George's father, George III, the marriage remained illegal in English law and he was forced by Parliament to marry Caroline of Brunswick in 1820.

The gifting of a miniature portrait of an eye was a perfect way of maintaining the anonymity of a lover or romance (fig. 4.31). The fashion for Lover's Eye jewellery spread throughout Europe and continued well into the 19th century. Many eye portraits of celebrities of the period still survive. Queen Victoria even briefly revived the tradition when she commissioned eye portraits of her beloved children as trinkets. Some of the Lover's Eyes bear poignant inscriptions such as 'Il ne voit et ne veira que toi' (He does not see me, he only sees you; fig. 4.32).

REGINA CORDIVM

5 The Nineteenth Century
The Age of Sentimentality

THE LAVISHNESS OF THE FRENCH monarchs and aristocracy in the 18th century played a significant role in accelerating the French Revolution between 1789 and 1799. The repercussions of this period of upheaval were felt throughout the next century in Europe, prompting political, economic and social change. The Industrial Revolution which began in the late 18th century was creating a middle class of wealthy industrialists and businessmen, an aristocracy of riches now competing with the old aristocracy of birth and property. Although royalty would continue to lead taste, the new distribution of wealth throughout society resulted in a higher demand for jewellery, and new industrial methods of production were helping make it more widely available and affordable.

This was also a period of cultural change. Romanticism, an intellectual movement in the visual arts, literature and music, had emerged across Europe in the late 1700s and was characterised by its emphasis on expressing personal feelings. This was reflected in the themes and imagery of jewellery, ranging from affection for family and friends, the passion shown for a lover, loyalty to a loved one or reigning monarch, and personal devotion and grief. For royalty, jewellery had always been a means of asserting power and political authority, but for the first time we also have an insight into the personal and sentimental jewellery they cherished. A number of royals also experienced a new celebrity status, becoming the style icons of their time for a wider population, not just the aristocracy.

Paris led fashion trends and styles for jewellery throughout the century. In the aftermath of the Revolution, Napoleon I (1769–1821) and his first consort Josephine de Beauharnais (1763–1814; fig. 5.1) brought splendour and a demand for luxury back to France. Napoleon fell passionately in love with the exotic Josephine, who hailed from an aristocratic family in the French colony of Martinique. His adoration is well documented in the many surviving letters he wrote to her from his numerous military campaigns. Josephine was already widowed with two daughters, Eugène and Hortense, when they met in the autumn of 1795

Fig. 5.1 ABOVE
Portrait of Empress Joséphine
by Robert Lefèvre
1806
Oil on canvas
Apsley House, The Wellington
Museum, London

OPPOSITE
Regina Cordium
by Dante Gabriel Rossetti
See fig. 5.33, page 103

Fig. 5.2
Engagement ring of Napoleon
and Joséphine with initials 'NB'
(Napoleon Bonaparte) and French
inscription: 'amour sincère'
(sincere love)
1796
Gold, enamel
Musée des châteaux de Malmaison
et de Bois-Préau, Rueil-Malmaison

and they were engaged by March 1796. Napoleon was then a mere general climbing up through the ranks, and the engagement ring he gave Josephine is quite unpretentious in comparison to the extravagant jewels he bestowed on her in later years (fig. 5.2).

A religious, rather than state, wedding ceremony took place a day before their coronation as Emperor and Empress of France in 1804. After a turbulent marriage they divorced in 1810, as Josephine was unable to provide an heir to the throne, but during their union Napoleon gave her permission to buy all the jewels she wished to match her wardrobe. Diamonds were his favourite and at his request had to be worn at all State occasions (fig. 5.1). Even after their divorce Josephine continued to commission large suites of jewellery, leaving Napoleon to pick up the bill as she was in debt. His love for her continued despite remarrying only months after their divorce.

The *corbeille de marriage* was a traditional basket of gifts presented by a groom to his bride. The one Napoleon gave Josephine in 1796 was an elegant urn made of silver and copper and covered with white silk. In 1810, as Emperor of France, he presented another *corbeille de marriage* in Vienna to Francis I, Holy Roman Emperor, when he asked for the hand of Francis' daughter Archduchess Marie-Louise of Austria (1791–1847). It was a sumptuous casket made by the goldsmith and cabinet maker Martin Guillaume-Biennais (1764–1843) containing jewels by Marie-Etienne Nitot (1750–1809), Napoleon's court jeweller and founder of the Paris jewellery house now known as Chaumet. Inside the casket were trays lined with white silk and filled with lavish jewels: a selection of rings, a diamond watch and parures (sets of matching jewellery) of cut steel, or set with sardonyx, coral, amethysts, malachite, shell cameos and more. Napoleon included a personal locket bearing his portrait and surrounded by diamonds. It can be seen in a portrait of Marie-Louise by Jean Baptiste Isabey, hanging from a diamond and ruby necklace which was part of a parure by Nitot (fig. 5.3). Napoleon also gave her a diamond parure of unimaginable grandeur and value, which included some major gemstones from the state Treasury, which had formerly belonged to Louis XIV, Louis XV and Marie-Antoinette.

In 1811, to mark the birth of their son and heir, the later King of Rome, Napoleon presented Marie-Louise with a necklace set with large diamonds commissioned from Nitot (fig. 5.4). It was traditional for royals and aristocrats to give diamond jewellery as a wedding present and gifts to mark the occasion of a birth. Napoleon's gifts of diamonds were as much a confirmation of his imperial status and authority as they were symbols of enduring love.

The wealthy middle classes of the period gave less opulent jewels as wedding gifts and substituted diamonds with more affordable gemstones, whose variety of meanings could be used to convey more complex sentiments. From the 1820s to the 1840s, Parisian jewellers became creative in keeping down the costs. They replaced diamonds with coloured gemstones, such as amethysts, aquamarines, chrysoprase,

citrines, yellow and pink topazes, and used garnets instead of rubies. Decorative filigree techniques such as *cannetille* (using tightly wound spirals and tendrils of gold wire or thin hammered sheets of gold) and *grainti* (granules) were ways of creating substantial pieces using less precious metal and reducing the price. The distinguished Parisian jeweller Henri Vever (1854–1942), who wrote on the history of French jewellery in the 19th century, describes these pieces as 'more spectacular than valuable'. One example is a parure from the 1820s or '30s made using the new filigree techniques and set with small rubies and diamonds (fig. 5.5). Gemstones associated with passionate love would have made the ideal wedding gift, especially with a centrepiece taking the shape of three red roses, a classic emblem of love.

Another example of love expressed through more modest means is a delicate Italian ring with a heart made of glass paste and underlying red metal foil imitating the ruby as a centrepiece (fig. 5.6). It has a band of tiny diamonds across the heart and is surrounded by tiny rubies and diamonds set in the crown and Cupid's arrows. The openwork hoop has the Italian inscription 'VI SON FIDELE' (You are faithful) expressing the wish of the bridal couple.

Rings are the most personal of all jewels and often conceal hidden messages in the ornament, such as one from Austria with diamond-studded billing doves forming the bezel and eyes made from ruby cabochons (fig. 5.7). Between the doves are three fruits, which may be apples, the attribute of Aphrodite, the goddess of love. The three apples may also represent the Three Graces, daughters of the God Zeus, who in Greek mythology were Aphrodite's attendants. They personify beauty, love and chastity, which relate to the bride on her wedding day.

A design frequently revived in love jewels of the 19th century was the serpent or snake, first seen in ancient classical jewellery. Especially poignant is the *ouroborus*, the serpent biting its own tail, creating a circle without beginning or end. It was used to symbolise eternal love and was a popular motif in bracelets, brooches and rings set with a variety of gemstones. For her engagement in 1840, Queen Victoria received from Prince Albert a serpent ring with emerald, diamonds and ruby eyes. Also popular were serpents set with turquoises, a gemstone traditionally associated with friendship and much favoured in the 19th century.

In combination with diamonds, turquoises would have signalled eternal true love (fig. 5.8). Their bright blue colour was reminiscent of forget-me-not flowers, which in the language of flowers signified loyalty and true love. At Queen Victoria's wedding in

Fig. 5.4 OPPOSITE
Diamond necklace, given by Napoleon Bonaparte to Empress Marie-Louise by François-Regnault Nitot, Paris
c. 1811–12
Gold, diamonds
Museum of Natural History, Smithsonian Institution, Washington DC

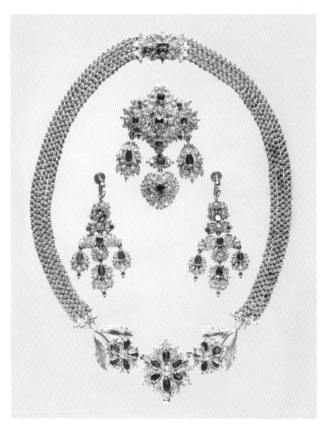

Fig. 5.5
A ruby parure with necklace, brooch and earrings
Probably France, c. 1820–40
Gold, rubies and diamonds
Private Collection

Fig. 5.6 RIGHT
Ring with crowned heart and Italian inscription
Italy, c. 1780–1820
Gold, silver, diamonds,
verre eglomisé
Alice and Louis Koch Collection in
the Swiss National Museum, Zurich

Fig. 5.7 FAR RIGHT
**Ring with billing doves flanking
three apples, the attributes of the
goddess Venus**
Vienna, 1866–72
Gold, silver, diamonds, rubies
Alice and Louis Koch Collection in
the Swiss National Museum, Zurich

Fig. 5.8
Serpent bangle
England, c. 1850
Gold, pavé-set turquoises,
diamonds
Private Collection

1840, the twelve bridesmaids were each given a brooch studded with turquoises and shaped like the Coburg eagle, in recognition of Prince Albert's family coat of arms. When the novelist Charles Dickens (1812–70) married his wife Catherine in 1836, he gave her a snake ring made of turquoise coloured enamel, diamonds and ruby eyes.

Amorous scenes with Cupids were numerous on jewels, usually depicted as *putti* in imaginative settings. An unusual pair of earrings of the late 19th century show Cupid in two different scenes painted against a pale blue enamel background (fig. 5.9). The enamel plaques are surrounded with diamonds and pearls, the classical combination of gems on wedding jewels. On one earring Cupid is riding a chariot drawn by swans and on the other by snails. Because of their beauty and grace, swans were the attributes of Venus, Cupid's mother, whose chariot was drawn by them in Roman mythology. Snails became love emblems due to their use of love darts in courting and mating rituals.

One of the characteristics of the Romantic movement that shaped culture in the 19th century was an interest in the natural world. In the early 1800s, extravagant and colourful jewels were crafted in the shape of flowers, leaves and fruits, conveying secret messages understood by the wearer and its giver. The rose, a flower sacred to Venus, was unsurprisingly one of the most popular flowers to be found in jewellery of the time. A ruby-studded rose can be seen on a ring dated 15 November 1831 (figs. 5.10a and b). It is unknown if this date was one of betrothal or marriage, or simply a declaration of love to accompany the lock of hair hidden in a compartment under the rose and presented as a token of love.

According to legend, Venus was injured by the thorns of a white rose which turned red with her blood, so the red rose became linked with the pains of love. Even today, the rose is one of the most recognisable love symbols. As envoys of love, flowers could not be more affectionately employed in a design as on a ring featuring alternating rose sprigs and daisies in enamel against an ornately engraved background (figs. 5.11a and b). The daisies conceal four little compartments bearing French inscriptions under the lids. Similar to the game played between lovers by plucking the petals of the daisy, they read 'je l'aime pas du tout' (I love you not), 'je l'aime un peu' (I love you a little), 'je l'aime beaucoup' (I love you a lot) and 'je l'aime passionement' (I love you passionately). In the language of flowers daisies stood for innocence.

The 18th century passion for plants and flowers continued into the 19th, reflected in the number and success of books outlining the language of flowers and their cryptic messages. The concept was well established in England. The playwright William Shakespeare (1564–1616) already mentioned over a hundred flowers in his plays and alluded to their meanings. The subject flourished in the 17th century and was revitalised in the 1700s when the Turkish delight in floral communication was introduced to England in 1717 by Mary Wortley Montagu (1689–1762), wife of the English ambassador to Turkey. In 1709 Lady Montagu wrote in a letter about floral messages 'There is no colour, no flower ... that has not a verse belonging to it; and you may quarrel, reproach, or send Letters of passion, friendship, or Civility, or even of news, without ever inking your fingers.' In the 19th century the most influential books on floriography were the *Dictionnaire du Language des Fleurs* by Austrian scholar Joseph von Hammer-Purgstall, published in 1809, and *Le Langage des Fleurs* by Madame Charlotte de la Tour (a pseudonym for Louise Cortambert) in 1819. Many similar publications followed, and it soon became popular to send secretive messages of love and affection or make flirtations with flowers. The individual meaning of each flower would have been understood by a lover, and in Victorian England it was a way of exchanging sentiments in a society where open communication was restricted by rigid etiquette.

Fig. 5.9
Pair of earrings with Cupid riding chariots drawn by snails and swans
France, c. 1880–1900
Gold, silver, diamonds, pearls, porcelain
Musée des Arts décoratifs, Paris

Fig. 5.10a and b
Ring with rose and concealed compartment containing a lock of hair
Germany, 1831
Gold, rubies, emeralds
Alice and Louis Koch Collection in the Swiss National Museum, Zurich

Fig. 5.11a and b OPPOSITE
Ring with roses and daisies, and compartments revealing French inscriptions
Probably Switzerland, c. 1830–40
Gold, enamel
Alice and Louis Koch Collection in the Swiss National Museum, Zurich

Fig. 5.12 LEFT
Friendship ring with pansy
France, 1819–35
Gold, enamel,
Victoria and Albert Museum, London

There was a widespread use of the pansy in love jewels, as it allowed for a play on words; the French word for pansy (*pensée*) had a second meaning of thought or reflection. It could serve as a rebus, for example on a ring of around 1819–38, where the pansy and the words 'à votre ami' can be read as 'Think of your friend' and was a romantic reminder of a loved one (fig. 5.12).

The wide selection of flowers and their meanings caught the imagination of jewellers. The jewel could appear to be as a simple adornment but transform into a message or secret between giver and recipient. A French brooch from a parure of 1860–70, which also includes a necklace, pair of bracelets and earrings, seems purely ornamental with its ivy foliage in green enamel and pearls. However, the parure is most likely to have been a marriage gift, with the ivy representing fidelity in marriage and the pearls symbolising chastity (fig. 5.13).

Fig. 5.13
Brooch with ivy foliage belonging to a parure
France (Paris), 1860–70
Gold, enamel, diamonds, pearls
Musée des arts décoratifs, Paris

A bouquet of naturalistically rendered flowers in varying shades of gold and worn as either a brooch or hair ornament carries a rather more complex message of love (fig. 5.14). The rose-buds signify love, or happy love, the pansies thoughts and the forget-me-nots true love. The butterfly hovering over the flowers represents Psyche, the wife of Cupid, as a symbol of perpetual love. This is sentimentality at its best, subtly expressed in a beautifully crafted gold brooch. Equally intricate is the message on a brooch/pendant with matching pair of earrings from around 1850–73, which show a dove with a sprig of myrtle, hovering over a nest with three eggs made of pearls, and framed by bright blue forget-me-nots. At first sight the scene appears unassumingly charming, however a more complex message can be unravelled, and hidden on the reverse behind glass is a lock of hair of a loved one (fig. 5.15).

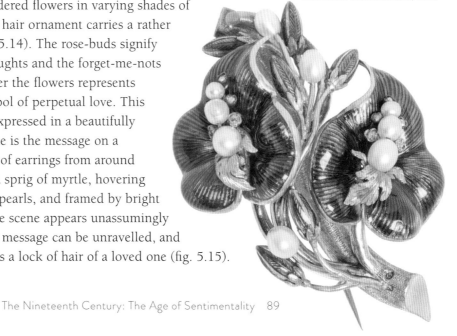

Fig. 5.14
Hair or corsage ornament with bouquet of roses, pansies and forget-me-nots
England, 1850
Rose, yellow and green gold, diamonds
British Museum, London

Fig. 5.15
Brooch with bird, bird nest and forget-me-not flowers, probably made by Harry Emanuel
London, c 1850–73
Gold, enamel, pearls
Victoria and Albert Museum, London

The myrtle is a bridal symbol, the dove evokes love, the pearls innocence and chastity and the forget-me-nots constancy and faithfulness. Not all messages on jewellery can be so easily interpreted. Inevitably some choices of design were personal to the couple and not always decipherable.

Complementing the use of flowers to express love and affection was the language of gemstones. Acrostic jewellery featured hidden love messages or poems spelled out using the initials of gemstones. Napoleon gave bracelets with acrostic messages to his family as wedding and birthday presents. They were made by his court jeweller Nitot,

Fig. 5.16
Acrostic bracelet with initials of gemstones spelling out 'amour'
Chaumet, Paris, c. 1890
Gold, silver, diamonds, amethyst, morganite, opal, uvite and rubies
Collection Chaumet, Paris

Fig. 5.17a and b
Ring with dog as a symbol of fidelity
Probably Switzerland, c. 1830
Gold, enamel
Alice and Louis Koch Collection in the Swiss National Museum, Zurich

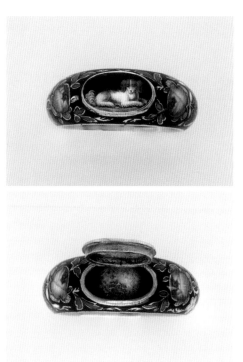

whose successor, Chaumet of Paris, has continued this tradition since the 19th century with the most popular word 'amour' (amethyst, morganite, opal, uvite and ruby; fig. 5.16).

In England, acrostic jewels could also signify 'love' (lapis lazuli, opal, vermeil, emerald) or 'regard' (ruby, emerald, garnet, amethyst, ruby, diamond). One heart-shaped English locket from around 1840 has 'regard' spelled out in stones on one side, and on the reverse, a forget-me-not flower made of turquoises and a ruby (fig. 5.18). The message is reinforced by a padlock mechanism with a key, suggesting the recipient holds the key to her lover's heart. Hidden inside the locket would have been a lock of her lover's hair.

Giving your loved one a lock of hair as a sign of affection had gained significance in the 17th century. By the 19th century, the age of sentimentality, such items were popular souvenirs both as love tokens or mourning jewels, expressing love beyond death. The hair was often concealed out of view in secret containers, for example in the bezel of a decoratively enamelled ring depicting a Cavalier King Charles spaniel, symbolising fidelity (figs. 5.17a and b). Accompanied by pink roses on either side it made a perfect token of friendship.

Secret compartments did not always hold a lock of hair. In the 1830s and 40s pendants or rings shaped like an envelope or purse would open like a love letter, to reveal surprise messages. These were highly fashionable. One ring shows a white rose against a dark blue enamel background and, when opened, reveals the word 'AMOUR' (figs. 5.19a and b). Another reveals a turquoise heart surrounded by foliage and a rose in different shades of gold (figs. 5.20a and b). More common was the word 'amitié' (friendship) which suggests these rings were romantic gifts, expressing feelings for someone special.

Love inscriptions took on many guises. A dainty ring with oval bezel flanked by two decorative roses in rose gold with green gold foliage (figs. 5.21a and b) has an inscription painted in black on white which reads 'Lis dans mon Coeur' (Read in my heart). The ring holds a secret only known to giver and recipient: the top of the bezel slides open to reveal a white heart against a blue background and a continuation of the love message 'l'amitié pour la vie' (friendship is for life). The true significance of this very personal message is unknown to us – was this ring given as a vow of fidelity, in friendship or marriage?

Fig. 5.18
**Heart-shaped locket pendant
with initials of gemstones
spelling out 'regard'**
England, c. 1840
Gold, turquoise, rubies, emerald,
garnet, amethyst, diamond
Victoria and Albert Museum, London

A curious love declaration appears on a ring with a miniature Galilean telescope with a converging and a dispersing lens (figs. 5.22a and b). This lens system was known from about the 1580s and developed further by the scientist Galileo Galilei (1564–1642). In the 18th and 19th centuries such miniature telescopes were integrated into all sorts of novelty items. This French ring, from about 1820, unusually combines science with love, and was most likely given to a man. Each lens is enclosed by a narrow frame in white enamel with italic script in black. The content of the French inscriptions relates to the lens type. The one surrounding the converging lens reads 'qui pourrait attirer mes regards ils sont fixer sur vous' (who could attract my attention which is fixed on you). Along the dispersing lens can be found 'de près et de loin je vous aime' (from near and from afar I love you). This personal dedication is both cryptic and poetic, and a true affirmation of love.

Fig. 5.19a and b OPPOSITE, TOP
Ring in the shape of an envelope, revealing 'AMOUR' (Love) when opened
France, c. 1840
Gold and enamel
Alice and Louis Koch Collection in the Swiss National Museum, Zurich

Fig. 5.20a and b OPPOSITE, CENTRE
Ring in the shape of an envelope, revealing turquoise heart when opened
France, c. 1830-40
Gold, turquoise
Alice and Louis Koch Collection in the Swiss National Museum, Zurich

Fig. 5.21a and b OPPOSITE, BOTTOM
Ring with French inscriptions
France, c. 1840
Rose, yellow and green gold, enamel
Alice and Louis Koch Collection in the Swiss National Museum, Zurich

Fig. 5.22a and b
Ring with Gallilean telescope lenses
France, c. 1820
Gold and enamel
Alice and Louis Koch Collection in the Swiss National Museum, Zurich

We have little surviving evidence of personal royal jewellery from earlier centuries, but much survives from this period. The story of how Queen Victoria (1819–1901) fell deeply in love with her first cousin Prince Albert of Saxe-Coburg (1819–61) is well documented. Their initial meeting, their engagement and wedding continue to fascinate us today. Their devotion was reflected in the many gifts they exchanged over the years to mark their anniversaries, the births of their nine children, Christmas and many more celebratory occasions. The gifts show their shared love of paintings, miniatures, sculptures and art, as well as jewellery whose value lay in their intimate messages. Prince Albert was fond of giving Victoria numerous jewels which he personally designed and commissioned from jewellers. Many of the jewels have survived and allow us to make a very personal picture of their love for each other. Their customs initiated a fashion for sentimental jewellery in England and France.

One of the first gifts Albert sent from Germany to his then fiancée was a gold brooch with orange blossoms made of porcelain (fig. 5.23). It was given in November

Fig. 5.23 RIGHT
Orange blossom parure belonging to Queen Victoria with wreath, two brooches and a pair of earrings
England, c. 1839–45
Gold, porcelain
The Royal Collection of Her Majesty Queen Elizabeth II

Fig. 5.24 OPPOSITE
Wedding portrait of Queen Victoria by Franz Xaver Winterhalter
1847
Oil on canvas
The Royal Collection of Her Majesty Queen Elizabeth II

Fig. 5.25 BELOW
Ring with medallions commemorating the marriage of Queen Victoria and the Prince Consort Albert
England, 1840
Gold, diamonds and enamel
Alice and Louis Koch Collection in the Swiss National Museum, Zurich

1839 just after she had proposed to him in Windsor. He wrote a letter stating 'I send you a trifle which came to me here and appealed to me on account of its sentiment. May you think with love of your faithful Albert when you take it into your hand.' They married on 10 February 1840, with Victoria in a white dress, launching the enduring fashion for white weddings, and wearing in her hair a wedding wreath of real orange blossom flowers (fig. 5.24).

Victoria notes in her journal that a portrait of her commissioned from the Court painter Franz Xaver Winterhalter (1805–73) was 'a surprise for my beloved Albert'. In it she wears a sapphire and diamond brooch (fig. 6.44) which he presented to her as a wedding gift a day before the ceremony. In 1845, he gave her a brooch with orange blossoms and matching earrings, and in 1846, for their wedding anniversary, a matching wreath made of velvet, gold, enamel and porcelain orange blossoms to complete the parure.

Albert took great interest in the symbolism of flowers and their meanings would probably have well known to him. The orange blossom as a symbol of chastity and innocence dates back to Ancient China when it was placed on the gowns of young brides. In the Victorian era

it symbolised fertility and everyone wished to follow the example of her Majesty on their wedding day. For those who could not afford real orange flowers, which were rare and expensive, wax models were produced as a worthy imitation. Queen Victoria's dress, made from Spitalfield silk and Honiton lace, was also hugely popular. Rings were made to mark the royal wedding with gold medallions depicting their profiles set in a dark blue enamel hoop with diamonds (fig. 5.25).

The orange blossoms lived up to their promise as Victoria had nine children before Albert's premature death in 1861. One of the most treasured of her jewels, and a reflection of their deep love, is a gold charm bracelet of sentimental value given by Albert on 24 November 1840, three days after the birth of their first child, Princess Victoria (fig. 5.26). At the birth of each of their other eight children a charm was added, each engraved with the date of the birth and containing a lock of their hair.

The tradition of commissioning bracelets as wedding jewellery by the landed and monied classes is specific to the 19th century. A bracelet made by Morel & Cie, another predecessor of the Paris jeweller Chaumet and an official supplier to Queen Victoria, shows the arms of the noble Russian Shuvalova family on the left, and on the right, those of the Vorontsov family, surrounded by green enamelled ivy and diamonds (fig. 5.27). Research into the family provenance continues, but it appears

Fig. 5.26
Queen Victoria's charm bracelet with lockets containing her children's hair
England, 1840-57
Gold, enamel, hair
The Royal Collection of Her Majesty Queen Elizabeth II

Fig. 5.27 RIGHT
Bracelet commemorating the marriage of Countess Elizaveta Shuvalova to Count Illarion Ivanovich Vorontsov-Dashkov by Morel & Cie
Paris, 1867
Gold, silver, diamonds, enamel
Schmuckmuseum Pforzheim

Fig. 5.28 OPPOSITE
Portrait of Empress Eugénie of France by Edouard-Louis Dubufe
1856-62
Oil on canvas
Château de Compiègne

Fig. 5.29 ABOVE
Empress Eugénie's heart locket
France, 1850
Gold, rubies
Private Collection

Fig. 5.30 BELOW
Empress Eugénie's diadem by Alexandre-Gabriel Lemmonier
Paris, 1853
Gold, silver, pearls, diamonds
Musée du Louvre, Paris

to commemorate the marriage of Countess Elizaveta Shuvalova to Count Illarion Ivanovich Vorontsov-Dashkov in 1867.

Empress Eugénie of France (1826–1920), a longtime friend of Queen Victoria, was considered the most stylish woman of her time and shaped fashion across Europe. In the 1850s she was pursued by Emperor Napoleon III, who was attracted by the beauty and grace of this Spanish princess living in Paris. He was renowned as a philanderer and Eugénie initially turned him down, like many of the women he proposed to. However, their engagement was finally announced in 1853 and the wedding ceremony took place barely two weeks later. Napoleon III claimed it was romantic love, but rumour suggested Eugénie had agreed to marry him because of his recent rise in status from President of France to Emperor of the French, and he knew that she would adamantly reject any advances from him without the sacrament of marriage. The union was deemed a success, even if over the years there was more affection between them than romance. Before the wedding, Napoleon had given her a three-leaf clover brooch set with emeralds made by the jeweller Jules Fossin (a partner with Morel). It appears in portraits of Eugénie (fig. 5.28), unlike the ruby-studded heart which he had hoped would reflect his affection (fig. 5.29).

At official occasions such as receptions and balls, Eugénie would wear magnificent gowns by the famous couturier Charles Worth adorned with the diamond-encrusted state jewels as a symbol of the legitimacy of her husband's reign. However, she was known to have preferred wearing her informal jewels, especially from her favourite

jeweller Mellerio in Paris. For the wedding, Eugénie was presented with a pearl and diamond diadem with 212 pearl drops and 1998 diamonds, made by the jeweller Alexandre-Gabriel Lemonnier (c.1808–84; fig. 5.30). Some of the gems were taken from a parure formerly belonging to Marie-Louise, Napoleon I's second wife.

Eugénie was infamous for her love of pearls, which she wore in multiple strands in unimaginable quantities and configurations, creating a fashion copied by the aristocracy of Europe. Napoleon III had given her pearls for their wedding, as was traditional. Madame Carette (1823–89), her loyal lady-in-waiting, wrote in her memoirs *My Mistress, the Empress Eugénie*: 'There is an old saying that the pearls worn by women on their wedding day are the symbols of tears to come. The Empress, however, did not then believe in superstition, and on that day wore a magnificent necklace of pearls over her satin corsage. But alas! The omen was in this case only too faithfully fulfilled; and after the war the Empress sold this necklace along with her other jewels.' Madame Carette was alluding to the fall of the French Empire in 1870 and subsequent exile of the royal family to England. In many countries it is still traditional to give the young bride pearls to wear at their wedding, alluding to their original symbolism as emblems of chastity, just as the white wedding dress indicates purity and innocence. However, in some countries, such as Italy, it is even today considered bad luck to give the bride pearls for her wedding.

In 1861, a formal, organised meeting between Princess Alexandra of Denmark (1845–1925; fig. 5.31) and the Prince of Wales, the future King Edward VII (1841–1910), led to a small, quiet wedding at St. George's Chapel in Windsor Castle, away from the press. The low-key nature of the event was in respect for Queen Victoria, then in deep mourning after Prince Albert's death. The marriage of their son and heir had been arranged by Victoria and Albert in the hope of bringing his wayward behaviour to an end. For the occasion of their wedding the Prince of Wales commissioned Garrard to make a suite of diamond jewellery: a 'very rich' brilliant diadem of large fine diamonds, a fine pearl and diamond cluster necklace with festoons of diamonds, a pair of earrings, two fine drop pearls and, to match, a fine pearl and diamond bracelet, as listed in the company ledger on 5 December 1862 (figs. 5.32a and b).

The page continues to describe many more jewels, such as a coral and diamond locket, amethyst pearl and diamond locket. No expense was spared; either the prince felt that the future Queen of England should be suitably bejewelled, since she lacked

Fig. 5.31
Her Royal Highness, Princess Alexandra of Wales
London, c. 1900
Photograph
Library of Congress, Washington DC

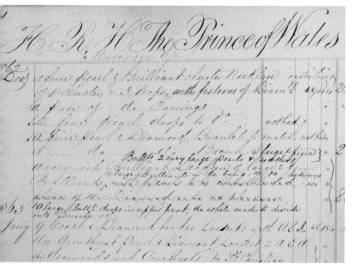

jewels of her own, or he was compensating for his liaison with an actress which he broke off just prior to the marriage. Edward VII continued his scandalous liaisons throughout their marriage, including a long dalliance with socialite Alice Keppel. Alexandra graciously commented that she understood the king's love for his mistresses, 'after all, he loved me the best'.

Nineteenth-century jewellery was not simply a story of royals, diamonds and pearls. During the second half of the century, the tempestuous relationships and love affairs among a group of British painters known as the Pre-Raphaelites challenged Victorian morality and the public perception of love in art. Their paintings of beautiful women, usually their muses or life partners, are depictions of extreme femininity and of human emotions such as unrequited, adulterous, tragic or illicit love. They are often transformed into mythical figures wearing jewellery infused with symbolic meanings. In 1860, the painter Dante Gabriel Rosetti married Elizabeth Siddall, a model, poet and artist in her own right, and commemorated the occasion in a portrait of her as *Regina Cordium* (The Queen of Hearts). The subject continued to preoccupy him after Lizzie's early death in 1862 and in 1866 he painted his long-time muse Alexa Wilding (1847–84) using the same theme (fig. 5.33).

The painting is full of love symbolism. There are roses in the foreground and the red-haired model wears gold chains with a heart-shaped pendant and holds a stem of irises representing purity or unrequited love. In the background is a cameo with a blindfolded Cupid holding a bow and arrow and a heart, symbolising desire and erotic love. Perhaps these were feelings for his deceased wife that the artist was unable to express in words.

Similar symbolism can be seen in the work of jewellers Castellani of Rome who were inspired by designs from classical antiquity. They created a gold ring around 1860–70 with a heart-shaped ruby lying in the palm of a hand (fig. 5.34). Ancient examples either holding an apple, pomegranate or shell referred to the attributes of Venus, the goddess of love. A mistletoe brooch made around 1880 by Carlo Giuliano, an Italian jeweller working in London, shows green enamelled leaves enclosing a berry of translucent moonstone with the carved features of an *amorino* or Cupid (fig. 5.35). In the Victorian era the mistletoe symbolised a kiss, and when worn, the sentiment 'kiss me'; the *amorino* embodied love.

Fig. 5.33
Regina Cordium
by Dante Gabriel Rossetti
1866
Oil on canvas
Kelvingrove Art Gallery and
Museum, Glasgow

Fig. 5.34 ABOVE
**Ring with hand holding a ruby
heart by Castellani**
Rome, 1860-70
Gold, ruby
Private Collection

Fig. 5.35 LEFT
**Mistletoe brooch with an
amorino's head by Carlo Giuliano**
c. 1880
Gold, enamel, moonstone
Private collection

6 From 1900 to Today
Diamonds continue to be a Girl's Best Friend

RARELY HAS JEWELLERY DESIGN experienced such changes and aesthetic diversity as in the 20th and 21st centuries. This is largely due to the remarkable shifts in society caused by global, political and economic circumstances, and rapid technological advances. Radios, telephones, cinematography and television, as well as the motorcar, aeroplanes and space age technology, have had an enormous impact on the way we communicate with one another. Today, computers and social media have revolutionised our daily lives. Despite all these advances in the ways love can be communicated, the simple act of exchanging jewellery between lovers remains a constant. Even though techniques for making jewellery have made huge leaps forward, and designs have adapted to contemporary fashions, the role of jewellery as an expression of love endures.

Traditions from earlier centuries have been adapted in accordance with modern practices and sensibilities. The wearing of white or cream virginal wedding dresses is still popular today, especially for church weddings, but the practice has not been constant since Queen Victoria first popularised it. In the early 1900s, conventions had begun to shift, and brides began wearing evening wear and, later, smart day wear in varying colours, especially when marriage vows were taken in a registry office. Over the decades wedding practices became less formal and conventional. By the 1920s, women were leading more active lives and often working; their increasing social and political independence undeniably factors in changing attitudes towards marriage, dress and jewellery.

At the start of the 20th century, however, Victorian values were still very much in vogue. The Belle Epoque period, from about 1890 until the outbreak of the First World War in 1914, was a time of peace in Europe, a 'golden age' when Parisian jewellers led taste. Splendour and elegance was at its highest levels for those who were privileged and wealthy. Diamonds were plentiful and had become more accessible and affordable after the discovery of new sources in South Africa in the 1870s. Advanced polishing and cutting techniques were developed by about 1900, which allowed for more sophistication and a mesmerising sparkle in the recently invented electric light. Platinum was valued for its whiteness and, above all, for its strength which allowed settings to be almost invisible, enhancing the light refraction on the intricate diamond cuts. The brilliant cut was fashioned with more facets and was followed by a profusion

Fig. 6.1
'Eglantine' necklace by Cartier
Paris, 1906
Platinum, gold, diamonds, emeralds
Cartier Archives

of fancy cuts, such as marquise, square, pear-shaped and even heart-shaped cuts. Diamond jewellery was worn in abundance and designs became ever more intricate, with silhouette-like settings for diamonds giving the gemstone great prominence.

Tiaras had made a comeback by 1900. Originating in the classical world, they had gradually lost their significance with the emergence of Christianity. It was not until the 18th century that they regained their earlier popularity and the wearing of a tiara became the prerogative of married women, a symbol of their status and having been 'queen for the day' at their wedding. By the early 20th century, tiaras were popularly given on the occasion of a wedding and formed part of the bride's *corbeilles de marriage*, or dowry, along with additional, and sometimes matching, sets of jewels. In 1907 an olive leaf tiara was made in Paris by Cartier for the marriage of Marie Bonaparte (1882–1962) to Prince George of Greece and Denmark (figs. 6.2a and b). The design choice of the olive branch was intentional. It was traditionally associated with Greece, alluding to the groom's heritage, but had also been linked to bridal traditions since Antiquity. Marie Bonaparte was descended from Napoleon I and was a psychoanalyst and author before her marriage elevated her to a royal life. The magnificence of her marriage jewels led to their display in Cartier's Paris windows.

Fig. 6.2a BELOW, LEFT
Olive-leaf wedding tiara worn by Princess Marie Bonaparte by Cartier
Paris, 1907
Platinum and diamonds
Cartier Archives

Fig. 6.2b BELOW, RIGHT
Princess Marie Bonaparte wearing her olive-leaf wedding tiara
1907
Photograph
Cartier Archives

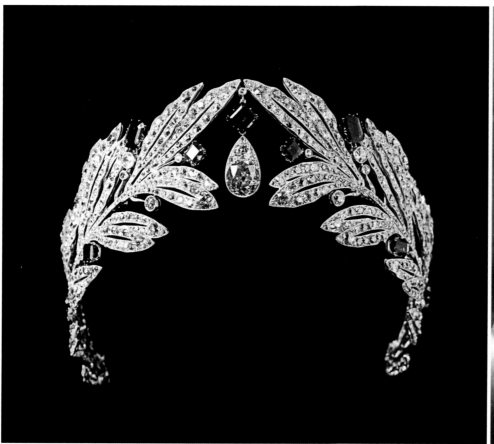

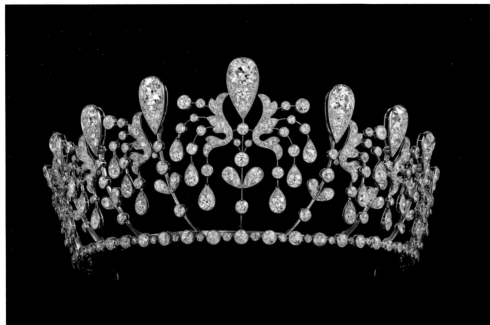

Fig. 6.3
Bourbon-Parma wedding tiara with fuchsia motifs made for Hedwige de La Rouchefoucauld by Joseph Chaumet
Paris, c. 1919
Platinum and diamonds
Collection Chaumet, Paris

A more romantic choice of motif can be found on a tiara featuring fuchsias, symbolising humble love, made by Chaumet in Paris. It was delivered on the morning of the wedding between Prince Sixtus of Bourbon-Parma, a descendant of Louis XIV of France, and Hedwige de La Rochefoucauld on 12 November 1919 (fig. 6.3). In this case the tiara was commissioned by the mother of the bride, Louise, Duchess of Dodeauville, in the new garland style of the period. It has almost imperceptible knife-edge platinum settings surrounding the diamonds which contribute to the brilliance of the gems.

The so-called 'Eglantine' necklace, almost wreath-like in appearance, is rich in love symbolism (fig. 6.1). It was made by Cartier in 1906 but its subsequent history has been lost. It features three dog roses graduating in size with buds and decorative foliage. The blossoms and leaves are densely studded with diamonds of different cuts and sizes in fine platinum settings, while emeralds set in yellow gold are interspersed within this embodiment of love and virtue. The necklace epitomises the newly-fashionable 'garland style', a term coined by Cartier and characterised by the decorative use of garlands made from ribbon bows, swags, tassels, laurel leaves, trellis or lace patterns. It consciously harked back to 18th-century Rococo designs and the stylish taste of Marie-Antoinette, Queen of France.

Even if not immediately discernible to the viewer, the choice of a particular flower dominates the symbolism and design of a watch made by Chaumet, Paris, thought to have been commissioned by a Marquis of Montesquiou in 1908 (fig. 6.4). The dainty watch with its blue enamelled frame is attached to a pearl bracelet by two diamond-set swags, each with a forget-me-not blossom in the centre. Hidden from view under

Fig. 6.4
Forget-me-not watch by Joseph Chaumet
Paris, c. 1908
Gold, enamel, platinum, diamonds, pearls
Collection Chaumet, Paris

the dial is a black and white photo of the giver, underlining the watch's secret love message to 'forget me not'.

The inventiveness of communicating secret love messages in jewellery appears to be limitless. The design of an English brooch from 1900, circular in form with three bands of translucent dark blue enamel over an engraved guilloché pattern and diamonds set in yellow gold, appears at first glance to be purely decorative (fig. 6.5a). However, the brooch hides a covert message of love only known to the wearer. When the two central discs are turned and the diamond studded ornaments aligned, the word 'CHERIE' (dear or sweetheart) is revealed (fig. 6.5b).

More modern and abstract in design was the popular concept of a pair of wings worn as brooches. They evoked Cupid's wings, a motif favoured by both French and English jewellers during this period. The brooches could also be adapted and mounted on an aigrette (a type of headdress) worn in the hair, such as the magnificent pair made by Chaumet, Paris, for the American heiress Gertrude Vanderbilt (1875–1942; fig. 6.6). In keeping with her bold taste for jewellery, the rows of finely set diamonds contrast with the curves of bright translucent blue enamel imitating sapphires. Vanderbilt was a student of sculpture under August

Fig. 6.5a and b ABOVE
Articulated brooch with the word 'CHERIE' (sweetheart) in diamonds
England, c. 1900
Gold, enamel, diamonds
Wartski, London

Fig. 6.6 BELOW
Cupid wing brooches by Joseph Chaumet
Paris, c. 1908
Platinum, gold, enamel, diamonds
Collection Chaumet, Paris

Rodin and the founder of *Vogue* magazine. Together with her extremely wealthy husband, Harry Payne Whitney (1872–1936), they founded the Whitney Museum of American Art in New York. Vanderbilt was a fan of Chaumet jewels and had, among other pieces, another pair of wings with rubies.

The arrow became a popular motif in the 20th century. Evoking Cupid's attribute, although usually designed without a heart or any other associated symbols, the arrow-shaped jewel was powerful in its message: whoever was hit by the arrow was struck by love. One example from 1918 is set with diamonds and invisibly set calibre cut sapphires (fig. 6.7). The symbolism of the gemstones would have enhanced the message of love.

Alongside the fashionable diamond jewels and the garland style, a new art movement had begun to affect jewellery design by the 1890s. Known as Art Nouveau in France, and the Arts and Crafts movement in Britain, it quickly spread to many other European countries, such as Austria, Germany, Spain, Denmark and the Czech Republic. Although it developed in distinct ways within each country, the ideals of the movements were similar. Arts and Crafts jewellers chose to use less valuable metals, not just silver but also brass, copper or even aluminium. Gemstones were chosen for their colour and symbolism rather than their monetary value; the jewellers' focus was on craftsmanship, rather than materials. With the concurrent revival of medieval styles, harking back to the craftsmanship of the individual goldsmith came a preference for gemstones in their natural cabochon shape, simply polished rather than faceted, and for the use of blister pearls with unusual shapes. One such example is a romantic corsage ornament/brooch of 1912 called the 'Love Garland' and designed by wife and husband Georgie (1866–1934) and Arthur Joseph Gaskin (1862–1928) from Birmingham (fig. 6.9). The brooch was made of silver with highlights of gold and depicts a garland of flowers surrounding an opal heart. It is set with lustrous opals, pink tourmalines, emerald coloured glass pastes, blister pearls and small daisy-like flowers in silver.

Reacting against industrially-produced jewellery of the 19th century, Arts and Crafts metalworkers intentionally left the marks from their hammer blows on their work as evidence of hand crafting. This is clearly visible on a belt buckle of about 1900 designed by Talwin Morris (1865–1911), made of chased and repoussé

Fig. 6.9
***Love Garland* brooch by Georgie**
Gaskin and Arthur Joseph Gaskin
England, 1912
Silver, gold, opal, pink tourmaline,
blister pearl, emerald coloured paste
Private Collection

Fig. 6.10 FAR LEFT
Honeysuckle ring, attributed to Antoine Beaudouin
Paris, 1900
Gold, enamel
Alice and Louis Koch Collection in the Swiss National Museum, Zurich

Fig. 6.11 LEFT
'The Betrothal – To Have and to Hold' ring by René Lalique
Paris, c. 1904
Gold, enamel, peridot
Private Collection

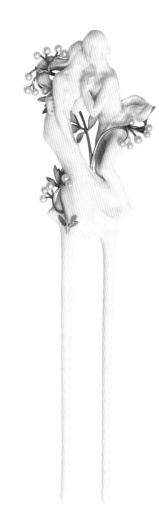

aluminium (fig. 6.8). He was known for metalwork, furniture and book designs in the so-called 'Glasgow style', featuring contrasting geometric lines and natural forms, as seen in the buckle's enchanting depiction of a pair of billing doves with interlocking tails. Despite the modest materials, the sentimental message is very expressive, especially with the recurring heart motif in green glass pastes.

The Art Nouveau style in France was an avantgarde movement and an important stepping stone towards Modernism in jewellery. Naturalistic subjects, such as the human form, plants, flowers and animals were transformed into highly decorative designs with sinuous, curvilinear forms celebrating life and love. A gold and enamel ring of 1900, attributed to the Paris jeweller Antoine Beaudouin, shows naturalistic honeysuckle flowers with intertwining foliage (fig. 6.10). The design appears merely ornamental, but in the language of flowers honeysuckle symbolised the bond of love, a message which would have been understood between the giver and recipient.

At the International Exhibition of 1900 in Paris, the French designer René Lalique (1860–1945), was hailed by critics as the 'emancipator and moderniser of French jewellery'. In 1904 he made a ring titled 'The Betrothal – To Have and to Hold' (fig. 6.11). Two black enamelled crows are perched on a gold twig facing each other and holding between their claws a triangular peridot gemstone denoting purity. Crows are known to mate for life, so the symbolism could not have been more appropriate for a betrothal or anniversary.

Also in 1900, the jewellers Paul and Henri Vever, from Maison Vever in Paris, created an ornamental hair comb, a highly fashionable ornament during the Art Nouveau period (fig. 6.12). The sculpted ivory figures represent the young lovers Daphnis and Chloe in an affectionate embrace, entwined by mistletoe made of translucent green enamel and pearls. In the language of flowers mistletoe means 'Kiss me'. The story derives from a Greek romance of the 2nd century AD by the author Longus. It was highly popular in the early 20th century, represented in romantic and erotic paintings and even in a ballet by Maurice Ravel which premiered in 1912.

Fig. 6.12
Hair comb with Daphnis and Chloe by Maison Vever
Paris, 1900
Gold, enamel, ivory, pearls
Musée des arts décoratifs, Paris

Fig. 6.13a and b RIGHT
**King and Queen of Hearts
clip brooches by Cartier**
1938
Yellow gold, enamel, diamonds
Private Collection

Fig. 6.14 BELOW
**The Duchess of Windsor wearing
her Cartier engagement ring**
Late 1930s
Photograph
Everett Collection

Fig. 6.15 OPPOSITE
**Cartier drawing of the Duchess of
Windsor's engagement ring with
emerald weighing 19.77 carats**
1936
Pencil and watercolour on paper
Cartier Archives, Paris

Throughout Europe, the catastrophic First World War (1914–18) and the Great
Depression which followed the Wall Street Crash of 1928 transformed national
politics and economies. Many European monarchies gradually lost their powers,
replaced by a growing number of republics and democratically voted governments.
Taxes were raised and wealth redistributed. The upper classes, especially the
nobility of the preceding period, were experiencing a new way of life, and the
role of jewellery as a visible display of authority was diminishing. War widows in
their millions needed to work outside the home and opportunities for women's
employment increased. The practicalities of work and transport, often by bicycle,
affected their dress: hemlines rose and fashions simplified, along with their choice
of jewellery.

Although hardly to be described as modest pieces, a pair of clip brooches designed
by Cartier of Paris in 1938 can be seen to represent how a more light-hearted
approach to design had affected even a high-end luxury jewellers (figs. 6.13a and b).
Made in yellow gold with enamels and diamonds, the Queen of Hearts holds a rose
in her hand and a bright red heart touches/caresses her cheek. The King of Hearts
clasps a sword which pierces a red heart. In a pack of playing cards, the suit of hearts
is associated with the season of Spring, emotion and love. These clip brooches would
have been worn by a couple as a sign of their affection for one another.

Despite this drift towards less ostentatious taste, examples of conspicuous
consumption of jewellery persisted. During the 1930s, a sensational romance
between the Prince of Wales, the future King Edward VIII (1894–1972, reigned
1936), and the twice-divorced American socialite Wallis Simpson (1896–1986)

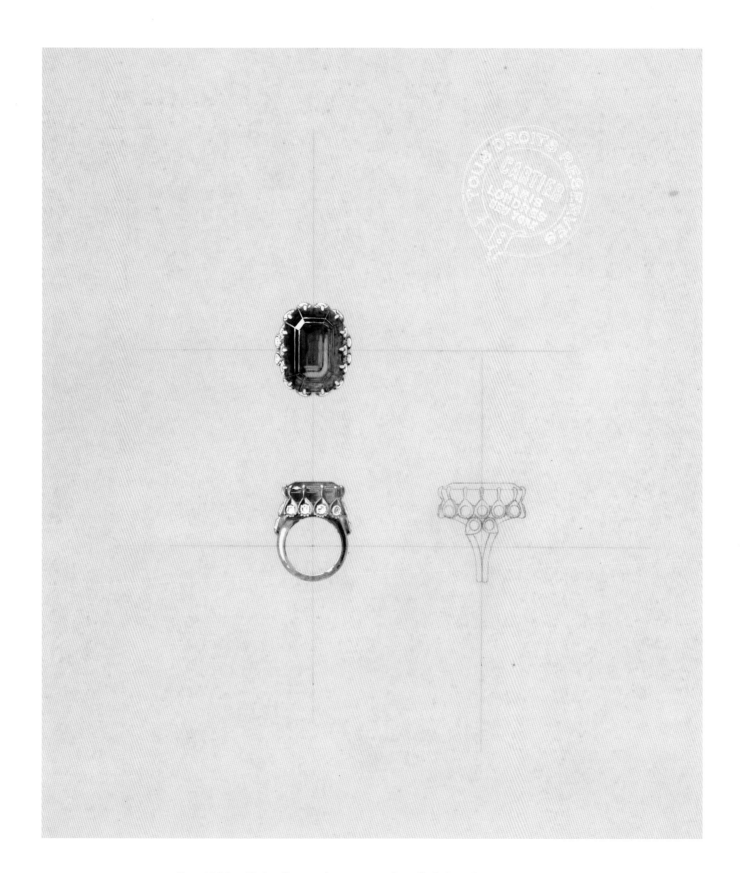

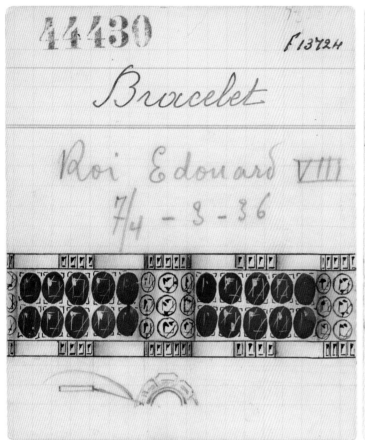

44430   F 13724

Bracelet

Roi Edouard VIII
7/4 – 3 - 36

28. 2. 36

Rubel Bracelet brillants ronds
rubis et brillants baguettes

030155/34740	28 rubis facel.	44.10	1800	79.380
	12 " "	17.92	1300	23.296
32170	48 brillants	7.78	850	6.613
Rubel	102 baguettes	15.02	1365	20.502
"	36 brillts ronds	17.59	1.770	31.135
"	frais de retaille (poids net 60.74)			235
"	Montine platine			18.420
	Frais generaux			17.958
				197.539

Fig. 6.16
Product card featuring the 'Hold Tight' bracelet by Van Cleef & Arpels given by Edward VIII to Wallis Simpson
Paris, 1936
Van Cleef & Arpels Archives

rocked the Establishment (fig. 6.14). They first met at a social event in 1931, where Mr and Mrs Ernest Simpson were flattered by the attention of the heir to the throne. When Wallis Simpson was first presented at Court without the company of her then husband, who was in financial distress, she borrowed a white satin dress and wore an aquamarine and crystal ornament and an aquamarine cross pendant, admitting in a letter to her aunt, 'These I need not add are imitations but effective.' By 1933, the dalliance between Wallis and the Prince of Wales had escalated into a love affair which would result in the abdication of Edward VIII in 1936, before his coronation. Edward, known to friends and family as David, followed his heart rather than the demands of his country, which he stated clearly in the radio broadcast announcing his abdication to the nation: 'But you must believe me when I tell you that I have found it impossible to carry the heavy burden of responsibility and to discharge my duties without the help and support of the woman I love.'

While still king, Edward had given Wallis an engagement ring by Cartier, made in gold with diamonds and a 19.77-carat emerald (fig. 6.15). Engraved inside the hoop was the inscription 'We are ours now'. He also commissioned from Van Cleef & Arpels

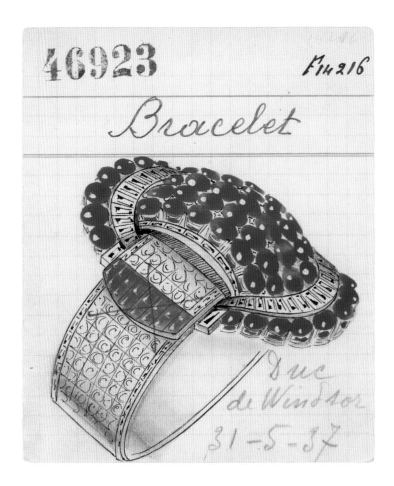

in Paris, a ruby and diamond bracelet inscribed 'Hold Tight' and the date '27 III 1936' (fig. 6.16). Such phrases as 'Hold Tight' or 'I am holding you tighter than ever' were echoed in the letters they exchanged before their marriage the following year.

By 18 May 1937 their marriage contract had been completed and an original design for a *jarretière* (garter) bracelet with sapphires and diamonds, also known as the 'marriage contract bracelet', was commissioned as a wedding gift for Wallis by the newly titled Duke of Windsor (fig. 6.17). The centrepiece consists of a large bow with cushion-set sapphires and baguette cut diamonds, the design possibly harking back to a true-lover's knot. Finally, on the 3 June 1937, they tied the knot in the Château de Candé in France and settled in Paris.

Over the years, the Duke of Windsor showered Wallis with sumptuous jewels from Parisian jewellers, foremost from Cartier, Van Cleef & Arpels, Suzanne Belperron, and David Webb in New York. The Duke of Windsor's wish that his wife's jewels should be dismantled after her death, as he felt they were too private to be owned by others, was never fulfilled. Instead, the Duchess of Windsor's collection was auctioned off in 1987, fetching immense prices.

Fig. 6.17
Product card featuring the *Jarretière* bracelet commissioned from Van Cleef & Arpels by the Duke of Windsor for his wedding to Wallis Simpson
Paris, 1937
Van Cleef & Arpels Archives

1937 was also the year a passionate love developed between two high-profile English actors, both already married to spouses who initially refused to divorce. At the time, adulterous relationships between members of the film industry had to be kept away from public view and press. It was not until August 1940 that Vivien Leigh (1913–67), who most famously played Scarlett O'Hara in the film *Gone with the Wind* (1939), and renowned theatre and film actor Laurence Olivier (1907–89) were able to marry. Their marriage lasted nearly twenty years, a tumultuous relationship and often emotionally rocky, but even after their divorce and subsequent marriages, they remained good friends. A simple gold band, thought to be Leigh's engagement or wedding ring, is engraved with floral decoration and is inscribed on the inside of the hoop in Olivier's handwriting: 'Laurence Olivier Vivien Eternally' (fig. 6.18). It may not be of great monetary value, but its message is expressive of the lifelong relationship between the two actors.

During the Second World War (1939–45), jewellers in Paris defied the constraints of the period and were as creative as ever, despite the shortage of metals and gemstones. Yellow gold substituted platinum and diamonds were replaced by colourful gemstones, which were applied sparingly. Despite the international crisis, demand for jewellery continued and designs became more playful. Jewellers such as Van Cleef & Arpels moved from Paris to the United States, opening boutiques first in Palm Beach in 1940 and then New York in 1942. During the 1940s they made

a series of enchanting love jewels: variants of prancing cupids holding a bow and arrow in yellow gold, with rubies as hair (fig. 6.19); a figure of the Shakespearean lover Romeo, and a collection of love bird compositions appropriately titled 'Les Inseparables' (fig. 6.20). These would have appealed during wartime, when sweethearts and families were separated by adverse circumstances. In difficult times the iconography of jewellery can be uplifting, and the wish to adorn oneself may even be more compelling.

In April 1956, a spectacular wedding took place between Prince Rainier of Monaco (1923–2005) and the famous American actress Grace Kelly (1929–82), then aged twenty-seven (fig. 6.21). It was a fairy-tale romance for the actress who had risen to fame within a few years of her first acting role in 1950. They first met in 1955 when she visited Monaco for a photo shoot at the Cannes Film Festival and the announcement of their engagement in January 1956 was a global sensation. At the press conference, Kelly revealed her ruby and diamond engagement ring – the gemstones of love but also the national colours of Monaco – and a 12-carat diamond ring made by Cartier (fig. 6.22). Grace Kelly made her last film, *High Society*, during the preparations for what was described 'the wedding of the century', and she is seen in the film wearing her diamond engagement ring.

During a stay in New York, the Prince sought advice at the jewellers Van Cleef & Arpels about a personal wedding gift for his fiancée. Hesitant about which gemstones would be appropriate for the occasion, he was guided and convinced by the jeweller Louis Arpels that pearls would be the most suitable for her delicate beauty and porcelain complexion. The wedding set consisted of a necklace, three-row bracelet, a pair of earrings and ring, made with cultured pearls, platinum and diamonds (figs. 6.23a–d). Only months later, Van Cleef & Arpels was named the 'Official Supplier of the Principality of Monaco'. The press published articles daily about the trousseau and wedding arrangements, and the ceremony was watched globally by millions. The American film studios MGM designed and created the wedding dress. Kelly brought glamour to Monaco and, as a fashion icon, created the 'Grace Kelly look': an understated elegance which was also reflected in her jewellery. Their love story ended tragically when the princess died in a car crash in 1982.

The life and loves of the American actress and singer Marilyn Monroe (1926–62), who became the sex symbol of the 1950s and continues to be a popular icon today, could not have been more different. Her films were highly successful, but her private life and three marriages were unhappy. In 1954 she married the retired baseball player Joe di Maggio, who, during their honeymoon

Fig. 6.21 ABOVE
Grace Kelly wearing her Cartier engagement ring in the 1956 film *High Society*
1956

Fig. 6.22 BELOW
Grace Kelly's engagement ring by Cartier
Paris, 1956
Platinum, emerald-cut diamond (10.48 carats), two baguette-cut diamonds
The Princess Grace of Monaco Collection, Palais Princier de Monaco

Fig. 6.23a,b,c, and d
Wedding set with necklace, bracelet, earrings and ring given to Grace Kelly by Prince Rainier of Monaco, by Van Cleef & Arpels
New York, 1955–56
Platinum, brilliant-cut, baguette-cut and navette-cut diamonds, cultured pearls
The Princess Grace of Monaco Collection, Palais Princier de Monaco

in Japan, gave her a single strand pearl
necklace of thiry-nine Akoya pearls from
Mikimoto, Tokyo, as a wedding present
(figs. 6.24a and b).

    The marriage lasted barely a year, but
di Maggio remained loyal to her even
after her death, regularly laying flowers
on her grave. In her films, Monroe
advocated glamour and jewels were in
abundance, most famously in the romantic
comedy *Gentlemen Prefer Blondes* (1953),
where she sang 'Diamonds are a girl's best
friend'. In real life she owned a few pieces of
costume jewellery but was particularly fond of
the Mikimoto pearl necklace, once stating that it
reminded her of happier times.

    Personal love was a very public affair for Elizabeth Taylor
(1932–2011), the British-born American actress whose career lasted six decades,
her seven marriages extensively featuring in magazines about Hollywood celebrities.
In an interview she described her marriages to Mike Todd (1909–58), an American
theatre and film producer, and to British actor Richard Burton (1925–84) as the loves
of her life. Both husbands are linked to her other passion, revealed in the title of
her 2002 book, *My Love Affair with Jewelry*. Taylor's famous collection of jewels was
auctioned after her death in 2011.

    Of the many pieces she owned, there are two sets of jewels which reflect her
happiest times. During her brief marriage to Mike Todd, between 1957 and his fatal

Fig. 6.24a
**Marilyn Monroe's pearl necklace
by Mikimoto**
Tokyo, 1954
Cultured Akoya pearls, white gold,
diamonds
Mikimoto America

Fig. 6.24b
**Marilyn Monroe wearing
the Mikimoto pearl necklace
given to her by Joe DiMaggio**
1954

Fig. 6.25a RIGHT
Elizabeth Taylor's ruby and diamond necklace by Cartier
Paris, 1951, altered in 1953
Platinum, gold, round brilliant-cut, baguette-cut and fancy-cut diamonds, eight cushion-shaped and oval faceted Burmese rubies
Cartier Paris Collection

Fig. 6.25b BELOW
Elizabeth Taylor wearing ruby and diamond necklace and earrings by Cartier
1957

Fig. 6.26a BOTTOM
Elizabeth Taylor wearing the Bulgari emerald and diamond necklace and earrings given to her by Richard Burton
Paris, 1968

plane crash in early 1958, she received many beautiful jewels, among them a set made by Cartier in 1951 featuring rubies and diamonds (figs. 6.25a and b). It was given to her, she describes, on 'a day of perfect love'. She continued in her book, 'When Mike gave me the rubies I was pregnant with Liza. We had rented a villa, La Fiorentina, just outside Monte Carlo, near St. Jean-Cap-Ferrat, about three months into our marriage. … Mike came outside to keep me company. I got out of the pool and put my arms around him. He was holding a red leather box, and inside was a ruby necklace which glittered in the warm light. It was like the sun, lit up and made of red fire. First, Mike put it around my neck and smiled. He then bent down and put matching earrings on me. Next came the bracelet. I just shrieked with joy, put my arms around Mike's neck, and pulled him into the pool after me.'

In 1962, during filming in Rome of *Cleopatra*, co-stars Elizabeth Taylor and Richard Burton fell in love. Cinecittà film studios were situated close to the famous jeweller Bulgari in the Via Condotti. They made regular visits and Burton lavished

Fig. 6.26b
Elizabeth Taylor's emerald and diamond ring by Bulgari
Rome, 1961
Platinum, emerald, diamonds
Bulgari Heritage collection

Fig. 6.26c
Elizabeth Taylor's emerald and diamond necklace by Bulgari
Rome, 1962
Platinum, 16 step-cut emeralds
(23.44 carats), emerald (60.50
carats), brilliant-cut and pear-
shaped diamonds
Bulgari Heritage collection

Fig. 6.27 ABOVE
Jacqueline Kennedy's 'Two Fruits and Leaves' brooch designed by Jean Schlumberger for Tiffany & Co.
New York, 1956
Gold, platinum, diamonds and rubies
Tiffany & Co. Archives

Fig. 6.28 BELOW
Ring with nuzzling doves perched on a nest by Ilgiz Fazulyanov
Moscow, 2017
Gold, enamel, diamonds, Akoya pearls
Private Collection

extravagant jewels on Taylor. He acquired a dazzling emerald and diamond brooch as an engagement present, soon followed by an emerald and diamond necklace with matching earrings and a wedding ring (figs. 6.26a, b and c).

Burton once said, 'I cannot see life without Elizabeth. She is my everything – my breath, my blood, my mind, and my imagination.'

Taylor admitted Burton gave her spectacular gifts for birthdays and Christmas but also used any excuse to give a piece of jewellery: 'He'd give me "It's Tuesday I love you.' They were married twice, first in 1964 until their divorce in 1974, and then again, for a mere six months, in 1975–6. In her many interviews, Taylor stated that their love was very intense, almost abnormally so, and that their personalities were demanding and temperaments explosive. They adored each other and remained friends after separation. The jewels are a legacy of a glamorous couple and passionate love.

Jewels are often given as a symbol of affection after childbirth. When their son John was born in 1960, Jacqueline Kennedy (1929–94) was given a jewelled clip by her husband John F. Kennedy, President of the United States 1961–3. It was in the form of ruby-studded fruits and diamond-set foliage and designed by Jean Schlumberger for Tiffany, New York (fig. 6.27). Jackie Kennedy, as she was known, was the daughter of a wealthy stockbroker. She met her future husband in 1952, marrying the following year. Her engagement ring was made by Van Cleef & Arpels and included a large emerald surrounded by diamonds in varying cuts. She became a role model in fashion and style, nicknamed 'Her Elegance' and was particularly famous for wearing multiple rows of (mainly fake) pearls.

The Moscow-based Russian jeweller Ilgiz Fazulyanov was given a special commission to create a set of jewellery for a client's wife, to mark the birth of their children. Renowned for his signature method of enamelling and his detailed observation of nature, Ilgiz created a stunning brooch (2013) and ring (2017; fig. 6.28) with nuzzling doves perched on a nest highlighted with diamonds and holding three pearls to symbolise the children in the family. Fazulyanov's fascination with the beauty of nature is clearly evident in his designs, especially in such details as the tree bark texture of the ring hoop, and the way he has captured the doves in a moment of affection. A message of deep affection resonates from this extraordinary composition. The brooch was shown in a major retrospective exhibition of Ilgiz's work at the Kremlin, Moscow, in 2016.

Doves, or lovebirds, are an attribute of the goddess Venus and appear in many guises. In 1961, Van Cleef & Arpels revived the style of the 1940s with a collection titled *Les Inseparables* (fig. 6.29). The lovebirds on this ring snuggle together back-to-back, their bodies covered with diamonds, the traditional gemstone of engagement and marriage, with beady eyes formed from rubies. The message of togetherness is conspicuous.

The heart, synonymous with affection and the seat of emotions, continues to be the most popular symbol of love. Contemporary jewellers are limitless in their imagination when employing it in their designs. Jane Sarginson of London specialises in designs with pearls. In 2003 she created an enchanting pendant, two centimetres in height, based on a naturally heart-shaped silvery-grey Southsea keshi pearl. She accentuates the colour of the pearl with a white gold frame and diamond surround (fig. 6.30).

Solange Azagury-Partridge, a London-based designer and jeweller, is mesmerised by the heart as a symbol of love and its religious significance as the Sacred Heart of Christ. Her designs can veer towards the anatomical, with titles such as 'Heart of Gold', alluding to the metal used, 'Bleeding Heart' made of red lacquer and 'Heart of Darkness', formed from blackened gold. Other collections such as *Tough Love* include the ring design 'On Fire', with a heart-shaped ruby, emerald or diamond, or the 'I do' ring with a diamond heart at its centre. Heated passion is expressed in a piece with the title 'Flaming Heart Ring', a heart-shaped black onyx with yellow gold setting, inlaid with a heart-shaped ruby surrounded by ruby 'flames' (fig. 6.31). The intensity of the red rubies against the black background is intentional: the heart is inflamed by love.

Utterly different in expression and concept is a carbon fibre heart suspended from a black leather strap, designed by the award-winning jeweller Fabio Salini of Rome (figs. 6.32a and b). The secret love message is only revealed when the two halves are opened. Inside are pavé-set diamonds on one side and on the other, rubies, with a pear-shaped ruby pendant emerging from the depths of the heart. The meaning of the jewel and its intimate message is only known to the wearer and giver.

Fig. 6.29
Love birds ring from the *Les Inseparables* collection by Van Cleef & Arpels
Paris, 1961
Platinum, gold, rubies, diamonds
Van Cleef & Arpels Collection

Fig. 6.30
Pendant with heart-shaped pearl by Jane Sarginson
London, 2003
18-carat white gold, South Sea Keshi pearl, diamonds
Private Collection

Fig. 6.31
'Flaming Heart Ring' from the *Cosmic* collection by Solange Azagury-Partridge
London, 1999
Gold, ruby, onyx

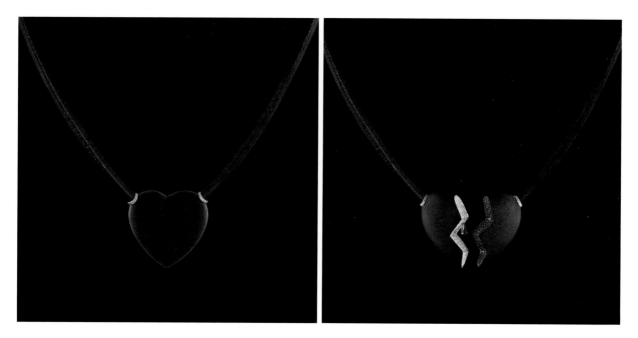

Fig. 6.32a and b
**Broken heart pendant
by Fabio Salini**
Rome, 2015
Carbon fibre, white and
blackened gold, rubies,
diamonds, leather strap.

Fig. 6.33a and b
**'Mythology Orb Locket Charm'
pendant by Annoushka**
London, 2018
Yellow, rose and white gold,
diamond

Fig. 6.34
**Bow knot ring from the *Insolence*
collection by Chaumet**
Paris, 2017
White and rose gold, brilliant-cut
diamonds

In 2018, a year of several royal weddings, London-based jeweller Annoushka launched a limited-edition jewel called 'The Mythology Orb Locket Charm' (figs. 6.33a and b). It is made of yellow and white gold and features the diamond-set crown-shaped bands characteristic of this jeweller. The design is inspired by the orb used in the royal coronation ceremony, an emblem of royal power and symbol of the cosmos. When opened, the orb locket reveals a high polished interior along with a tiny 18-carat rose gold heart, the symbol of love.

In 1995, the heart appeared in a more conceptual context, with ironic undertones, in a series of necklaces designed by Otto Künzli, a Swiss artist jeweller and former professor at the Akademie der Bildenden Künste in Munich (fig. 6.35). The gold pendant tube, heart-shaped in cross section, can be cut to a desired length, which gives each necklace its own title, such as '1cm of Love'. During this period Künzli also designed the 'Rolling Heart' and an object called '1 Meter of Love'. He explained, 'Trying to measure our deep feelings with the metric system is as paradoxical as cutting 10cm from infinity. And yet we tend to question the intensity of love occasionally and to assure each other of it time and time again. Now, being able to buy as if from a butcher's as much "heart sausage" as love is worth to us, or our purse allows, intimates that irony is also part of the mix here...'

Chaumet's collection *Insolence*, launched in Paris in 2017, plays with the concepts of tradition and irreverence (fig. 6.34). In a ring from the collection, the bow motif, with all its historically symbolic sentiments, and the steadfast knot, associated with marriage and 'tying the knot', are given a modern twist. Featuring a large diamond, the asymmetrical bow is complex in design and appears impossible to untie, but the intention of the designer is slightly cheeky. As described by Chaumet, 'Insolence tells the story of a diamond ribbon and a rose gold rope chain that meet to intertwine, tie and untie in a whimsical game of duality. A classic at first glance, this jewellery tale reveals a free-spirit. The bow-knot, on the verge of being undone, evokes light-hearted transgressions. Spontaneous and carefree, the "Insolence" collection celebrates a femininity which is sensual, hedonistic, and ready to embrace all of life's pleasures.'

Hong Kong jewellery artist Wallace Chan, known worldwide for his philosophical and fantastical approach to jewellery design, created a pair of earrings entitled 'Wheels of Love' (fig. 6.37). Love is seen here in a wider context. For Chan: 'The wheel is a carrier of meanings throughout human history. It tells us about time or space, the four seasons, phases of the moon, the zodiac and many more. The wheel symbolizes the cycles of life, it is one of the forms of the natural law, a microcosm of the universe and a token of eternity. In our daily life we have the wheel, and in our myths and imagination, too. Its form alone conveys motivation, making progress and moving forwards. The first wheel in human history appeared as early as 6000 years ago.' Chan describes the design of his earrings as a combination of two circular forms, the wheel and the tree ring. At the top of each earring is a flamingo flower which represents peace (emerald green) and passion (ruby red). The wheel pendants below are composed of six layers of gemstones – emeralds, rubies, diamonds, yellow diamonds, opals and lapis lazuli – forming two dazzling colourful swirls. To Chan, they are 'a pair of energetic objects flying across the universe, drawing star trails in the sky as it travels by'. The design brings to mind the lyrics of a love song by Emmylou Harris with the same title as the earrings, released in 1990: 'The wheels of love turn around and around'.

One of the most iconic designs of 20th-century love jewellery, which continues to inspire collections in the 21st century, is the 'Love Bangle' designed in 1969 by Aldo Cipullo (1935–84) for Cartier (fig. 6.36). Cipullo was an Italian-American jewellery designer who liked to subvert everyday objects with humour and affection. The original bangle comprised two semi-circles and was fastened around the wrist by screws, using the tiny gold screwdriver that came with it. It was almost impossible to put on by oneself and was therefore intended to be acquired only as a gift for a true love, offering eternal love at the turn of a screw. It was intended to be worn by men as well as women, and the screwdriver could be worn as a necklace by the partner, the 'keeper of love' of whoever wore the bracelet. Celebrity couples such as Elizabeth Taylor and Richard Burton, Sophia Loren and Carlo Ponti, Nancy and Frank Sinatra, Steve McQueen and Ali MacGraw, as well as the Duke and Duchess of Windsor, owned one of these iconic bangles.

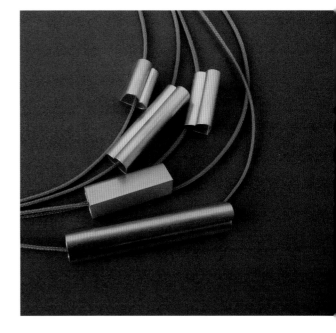

Fig. 6.35
'1cm of Love' by Otto Künzli
Munich, 1995
Gold 900, cord
Private Collection

Fig. 6.36
'Love Bangle'
Designed by Aldo Cipullo
New York, 1969
Gold

Relaunched by Cartier in 2012, the design has been simplified, with diamonds and other decorative features added, and continues to be exchanged by celebrities.

In today's age of the internet and social media, our culture is visually orientated. Smartphones are used to send messages in a slang of their own, with abbreviated language and emoticons, and tattoos are a must-have among the young generation. It is therefore unsurprising that some jewellers have transformed love jewellery; instead of employing symbolism to decode, the message is explicit and worn for all to see.

Mikimoto, a Japanese company based in Tokyo with stores worldwide, is known as the originator of the cultured pearl, which it has sold since 1893. The founder, Kokichi Mikimoto (1858–1954), adopted a motto which came true: 'I would like to adorn the necks of all women of the world with pearls.' By developing a new technique of growing cultured pearls, he made them more affordable. A strand of pearls was and continues to be a popular bridal gift in most countries. In 2013 Mikimoto launched the *Love Collection* as Valentine's gifts, or for any romantic occasion, and described these jewels as 'Young, fashionable and fun, this is the perfect romantic gesture' (fig. 6.38). Here, the word 'love' was formed of rose or

Fig. 6.37 OPPOSITE
'Wheels of Love' earrings
by Wallace Chan
Hong Kong, 2016
Emeralds, rubies, diamonds, yellow diamonds, opals, lapis lazuli
Private Collection

Fig. 6.38 ABOVE
Love Collection **by Mikimoto**
Tokyo, 2013
White gold, Akoya pearls with pink blush, pink sapphires

Fig. 6.39
Pendants from the *Memoirs*
collection by Shaun Leane
London, 2008
White gold, yellow gold, ink on
parchment

white gold and the letter 'o' set with a Japanese Akoya cultured pearl with pink blush. Under each word was suspended a pink sapphire, underlining the message. The London-based jeweller Shaun Leane, who started his career in Hatton Garden and is also known worldwide for his collaboration with the fashion designer Alexander McQueen, has said, 'I admire the past masters who – with their style and craftsmanship – created fine jewellery that was distinctive of its time. I like to fuse elements of tradition with a contemporary design approach. We cannot look to the future of design without remembering our past.' This he certainly achieved with his so-called 'Messenger' pendants from the *Memoirs* collection, which are based on sentimental Victorian jewellery, particularly mourning jewellery, but have a truly contemporary feel (fig. 6.39). They are cylindrical in shape, made of white and yellow gold occasionally set with diamonds, with a personal message or date enamelled around the barrel which might commemorate a new life, death or a special occasion. Unknown to the viewer, the pendant conceals a wound up scroll inside which bears a message to a loved one, for example 'Together forever', or very occasionally the ashes of a beloved. Each piece in this collection is inspired by personal contact with the client and their memories.

Stephen Webster is a multi-award winning and globally renowned London jeweller who also runs the workshop for the jewellers House of Garrard (founded in 1735). His collection *I Promise to Love You* was inspired by a forty-year friendship with the artist Tracey Emin and their artistic collaborations, particularly the handwritten messages transformed into neon lighting that she has created since the 1990s. One of her collections shares the same title. Webster's collection consists of necklaces, bracelets and earrings, either in gold, titanium or silver, bearing the image of a heart or a cross for a kiss and handwritten texts in italics. He uses mottos such as 'Love', 'More Passion', 'With You I breathe' and 'I promise to love you', as is visibly highlighted in diamonds on a wide cuff (fig. 6.40).

Marilyn Monroe's signature song 'Diamonds are a girl's best friend' is a slogan firmly rooted in our minds and imagination, and a concept which appears in many advertising campaigns for jewellers. Diamonds have an allure like no other stone and, as this book has shown, they have been linked with betrothals and weddings for many centuries.

In 1886, Charles Lewis Tiffany of New York transformed the style of the engagement ring when he created what is known today as the Tiffany setting. The diamond was positioned on a plain gold band and held by prongs in a high open setting, allowing the light to pass through the stone and enhance its sparkle. Today we describe this as a solitaire ring, and it is probably the most popular type of engagement ring. It was said that Tiffany, who masterminded

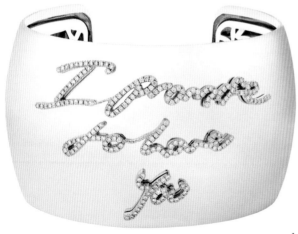

Fig. 6.40
Silver cuff with inscription
I promise to love you
by Stephen Webster
London, 2016
Silver, gold, diamonds

the design, believed that his American clients associated the diamond with royalty and pomp rather than fidelity and constancy. Nevertheless, the solitaire diamond ring was to become an iconic symbol of commitment to marriage. Other famous jewellers in the United States and Europe soon followed and promoted the diamond engagement ring as an idea rather than as a brand.

After the Wall Street Crash in 1929 and the ensuing global Depression in the 1930s, diamonds had become scarce and demand was slipping. De Beers, the diamond company who had exclusive control over the mines in South Africa and over all aspects of the trade worldwide, recruited New York advertising agency N.W. Ayer to reinvigorate the trade. They were to promote diamonds as a symbol of romance and encourage men to give their bride-to-be a diamond engagement ring which would not only be a measure of their love but also a reflection of their prosperity. In 1947, Ayer came up with the slogan which De Beers has continued to use ever since, 'A Diamond is Forever', possibly the inspiration behind the title of the 1971 James Bond film *Diamonds are Forever*. By the 1950s, the ad campaign had proved to be an enormous success in the trade and became a symbol of enduring love in popular culture.

Society photographers, newspapers and magazines recognised the audience demand for, and potential worth of, stories around royalty, movie idols and singers. Romance, engagements and gifts of diamonds between the rich and famous created a frenzy. Such stories were selling points for the publisher and, for the reader, dreams to aspire to. The desire to see glittering gemstones on a celebrity's hand has never ceased, and today they are even more in the limelight through the excesses of social media. Celebrities continue to influence and inspire the choice of engagement ring. In the 21st century, rather than going to the family or high street jeweller, many now choose to purchase their ring on the internet after researching styles, prices and the various qualities of diamonds at their own leisure. Diamonds continue to be timeless symbols of commitment to marriage.

The fascination for British royal weddings remains unabated, with such events watched by millions, if not billions, worldwide. The wedding of Princess Elizabeth and Philip Mountbatten, Duke of Edinburgh, on 20 November 1947 (fig. 6.41), was one of the earliest to be broadcast by radio, reaching 200 million listeners, quite an achievement at a time when televisions were still a luxury to possess.

Fig. 6.41
Official engagement photograph of Princess Elizabeth and Lieutenant Philip Mountbatten
London, 1947

Fig. 6.42 ABOVE, LEFT
Official engagement photograph of Prince William and Kate Middleton (future Duke and Duchess of Cambridge) with Diana, Princess of Wales' engagement ring
2010

Fig. 6.43 ABOVE, RIGHT
Diana, Princess of Wales, wearing her engagement ring with 12-carat blue Ceylon sapphire and diamonds, commissioned by Charles, Prince of Wales and made by Garrard, London
1981

Fig. 6.44
Brooch given by Prince Albert to Queen Victoria the day before their wedding in 1840

The Queen's engagement ring was made by the London jeweller Philip Antrobus, from diamonds taken from a tiara given by Prince Philip's mother, Princess Andrew of Greece: a 3-carat brilliant cut diamond accompanied by two smaller diamonds on either side. The gemstones may be small, but the ring is symbolic of a marriage which celebrated its 70th anniversary in 2017.

Another royal engagement ring steeped in history is that of Catherine, Duchess of Cambridge (formerly Kate Middleton), which was given to her by Prince William when he proposed in 2010 (fig. 6.42). The ring originally belonged to his mother Diana, Princess of Wales, presented to her by Charles, Prince of Wales, when he proposed in 1981 (fig. 6.43). Prince William explained his choice in an interview for ITV: 'It's my mother's engagement ring, and it's very special to me now, as Kate is special to me now as well. It was only right that the two were put together.' The sapphire and diamond ring was made by the royal jewellers Garrard and chosen by the Prince of Wales. The design goes back to a brooch given by Prince Albert to Queen Victoria the day before their wedding, made to his design by Garrard (fig. 6.44). The tradition lives on and the design continues to be a favourite. Indeed, it has become a trademark for the House of Garrard that every engagement ring they sell has a tiny sapphire set inside the hoop (figs. 6.45 and 6.46).

The memory of Princess Diana lives on in the engagement ring Prince Harry gave to Meghan Markle when he proposed to her in 2017 (figs. 6.47a and b). He was personally involved in designing the ring, made by London jewellers Cleave and Company, which incorporates an ethically-sourced diamond from Botswana, where the couple had travelled to several times. The two diamonds on either side are from a brooch which belonged to his mother, Diana, Princess of Wales, and his thoughts were similar to those of his brother: 'The little diamonds on either side are from my

Fig. 6.48
Lady Gaga at the 60th Annual
GRAMMY Awards wearing
a pink sapphire and diamond
engagement ring
2018

mother's jewellery collection to make sure that she is with us on this crazy journey together.' In recent years, jewellers have noticed an increase in couples being directly involved in the process of choosing and personalising their choice of ring.

The marriage of fashion designer Victoria Beckham, formerly a member of pop group the Spice Girls, and footballer and fashion icon David Beckham, has produced an extraordinary collection of rings, all of which she has worn individually on her wedding finger. When David proposed in 1998, her engagement ring was made of a 3-carat marquise cut diamond designed by Boodles, a leading diamond jeweller since 1798. As wedding gifts, they gave each other a Rolex watch. Most recently, she was spotted wearing her 14th ring on her wedding finger, a yellow square cut diamond. Her collection includes rings featuring a pear cut diamond, exceptional ruby, sapphire and emerald stones and many fancy coloured diamonds.

Many of the high jewellers today offer an array of diamond colours, such as yellow and pink diamonds set either as a solitaire, or in unconventional compositions and combined with white diamonds, like the 'Toi et Moi' ring by Bulgari (fig. 6.49) and the 'Gemini' ring by Boodles (fig. 6.50). In 2018, Lady Gaga, the American singer and songwriter, was rumoured to be secretly engaged to Christian Carino when she was seen flashing an oval-shaped pink diamond surrounded by white diamonds (fig. 6.48). An earlier engagement ring worn by the singer consisted of a large heart-shaped diamond.

In 2014, the American actor and director George Clooney astounded the public with the news that he was going to marry the Lebanese born Amal Alamuddin, an international human rights lawyer. When visiting her family in Dubai, he proposed with a ring he had helped design which featured a large ethically-mined 7-carat emerald-cut diamond with two tapered baguette diamonds set on the sides (fig. 6.51). The world's media descended on Venice that same year for their memorable wedding attended by A-list celebrities. The paparazzi were waterborn and used drones to catch a glimpse of the guests and the sparkle.

In keeping with modern sensibilities, George Clooney is seen wearing a wedding ring, a slim platinum band, while his wife Amal wears a pavé-set diamond wedding ring. Interestingly, although Prince Harry exchanged wedding rings with his wife, his brother Prince William chose not to wear one. The Canadian singer Michael Bublé proudly presented his wedding ring to the press in 2011 when he married Luisana Lopilato. When the globally renowned British singer Ed Sheeran was seen wearing a plain silver band in early 2018, the press speculated that he had married in secret, but he revealed it was an engagement ring that his fiancée Cherry Seaborn had made for him from silver clay (fig. 6.52).

No doubt he would have been amused by the media attention it had triggered but it shows how traditions are engrained in today's culture, despite trends to break away from tradition. Opinion is growing about whether a man can also wear an

Fig. 6.49
'Toi & Moi' ring by Bulgari
Rome, c. 1972
Gold, triangular-cut fancy vivid blue diamond (10.95 carats), triangular-cut white diamond (9.87 carats), baguette-cut diamonds

Fig. 6.50
Pink and white diamond 'Gemini' ring by Boodles
London, 2013
White gold, rose gold, pink diamonds, white diamonds

engagement ring – sometimes known as a 'management' or 'mangagement' ring – and show his commitment.

When same sex marriage was legalised in a number of countries, there was an increasing demand of engagement rings for men. The British jeweller H. Samuel launched a range of male engagement and wedding rings in 2009, and some jewellers such as Tiffany advertise 'couples' rings which can be worn by men and women. Similarly, Niessing, a company in Vreden, Germany, which was founded in 1873, have become known for their unisex wedding rings. Since the 1950s, they have developed an international reputation for their modern take on wedding bands, created by renowned designers and designed to be worn by both men and women. The materials they use range from white and yellow gold to platinum and titanium in innumerable combinations and with textured surfaces; the choice is vast. *Fusion*, a collection launched in 2005 by Niessing with the strapline 'Two Hearts One Soul', uses platinum and gold in the characteristic alloys developed by the firm (fig. 6.54). The title is self-explanatory, as it is for the *Duett* collection introduced in 1998, featuring interchangeable platinum and gold bands which swivel to reveal a tiny diamond (fig. 6.55).

A novel approach to friendship, engagement or wedding rings is seen in pieces made by the Munich artist jeweller Gerd Rothmann in his signature style. On the bezel he uses casts of the fingerprints of the couple to be married (fig. 6.53), each receiving the other's print.

The Biojewellery project, developed in 2005–7 by the jewellery designer Nikki Stott and Dr Ian Thompson from King's College, is very unusual and may offer a glimpse into the future of jewellery design. They created rings made from samples of cells from the teeth of the couple to wed. Living tissue was grown in a laboratory

Fig. 6.53
Couple rings, each bearing the
fingerprint of the other partner,
by Gerd Rothmann
Munich, 2005
White gold
Private Collection

and then combined with precious metals, with each ring containing the tissue of their partner – a very personal approach.

Alongside bold and unexpected new approaches to jewellery design, social norms continue to be challenged. The expectations of earlier generations that partners meet at a young age, marry, start a family and stay together forever, are being questioned. The so-called Millennial age group have different views about love and the patterns of life. What does not seem to be disputed, however, is the continuing appeal of jewellery to communicate and celebrate love in all its forms, a common desire which has endured since prehistory.

Fig. 6.54 ABOVE
Fusion ring by Niessing
Vreden, 2005
Gold, platinum

Fig. 6.55 BELOW
Duett ring by Niessing
Vreden, 1998
Gold, platinum

Index

Select Bibliography

Bayer, Andrea (ed.), *Art and Love in Renaissance Italy*, Metropolitan Museum of Art, New York. Yale University Press, New Haven and London, 2008

Bernstein, Beth. *If These Jewels Could Talk: The Legends behind Celebrity Gems*, ACC Art Books, Woodbridge, Suffolk, 2015

Boettcher, Graham C. *The Look of Love: Eye Miniatures from the Skier Collection*, Birmingham Museum of Art, Birmingham, Alabama, 2012

Camille, Michael. *The Medieval Art of Love*, Harry N. Abrams, New York, 1998

Campbell, Marian. *Medieval Jewellery in Europe 1400-1500*, V&A Publishing, London, 2009

Chadour, Anna Beatriz. *Rings: The Alice and Louis Koch Collection*, 2 vols., Maney & Sons Ltd, Leeds, 1994

Chadour-Sampson, Beatriz with Bari, Hubert. *Pearls*, V&A Publishing, London, 2013

Chaille, François. *The Cartier Collection: Jewelry*, Flammarion, Paris, 2019

Church, Rachel. *Rings*, V&A Publishing, London, 2011

Culme, John and Rayner, Nicholas. *The Jewels of the Duchess of Windsor*, Thames and Hudson in association with Sotheby's, London, 1987

Diamonds and the Power of Love: The Diamond Engagement Ring, A Commitment to Love over the Centuries, Diamond Trading Company, London, 2002

Ferris, Iain. *The Mirror of Venus. Women in Roman Art*, Amberley Publishing, Stroud, Gloucestershire, 2017

Gere, Charlotte and Rudoe, Judy. *Jewellery in the Age of Queen Victoria: A Mirror to the World*, British Museum Press, London, 2010

Grootenboer, Hanneke. *Treasuring the Gaze. Intimate Vision in Late Eighteenth-Century Eye Miniatures*, University of Chicago Press, Chicago and London, 2012

Hall, Edwin. *The Arnolfini Betrothal: Medieval Marriage and the Enigma of Van Eyck's Double Portrait*, University of California Press, Berkeley, 1994

Haugland, Kristina H. *Grace Kelly Style*, V&A Publishing, London, 2010

Heilmeyer, Marina. *The Language of Flowers. Symbols and Myths*, Prestel, Munich, London and New York, 2001

Levi, Karen (ed.). *The Power of Love: Six Centuries of Diamond Betrothal Rings*, Diamond Information Centre, London, 1988

Loyrette, Henri. *Chaumet: Parisian Jeweler since 1780*, Flammarion, Paris, 2017

Marchesseau, Daniel and others. *Bijoux romantiques 1820-1850: la parure à l'époque de George Sand*, Musée de la vie romantique, Paris, 2000

Marsden, Jonathan (ed. and introduction). *Victoria & Albert: Art & Love*, Royal Collections Publications, London, 2010

Seidel Menchi, Silvana (ed.). *Marriage in Europe 1400-1800*, University of Toronto Press, Toronto and London, 2016

Meylan, Victor. *Van Cleefs & Arpels: Treasures and Legends*, Antique Collector's Club, Woodbridge, Suffolk, 2015

Meylan, Victor. *Bulgari: Treasures of Rome*, ACC Art Books, Woodbridge, Suffolk, 2018

Munn, Geoffrey. *Triumph of Love: Jewelry 1530-1930*, Thames and Hudson, London, 1993

Munn, Geoffrey. *Tiaras: A History of Splendour*, Antique Collector's Club Ltd., Woodbridge, Suffolk 2001

Murray, Jacqueline (ed.). *Love, Marriage and Family in the Middle Ages: A Reader*, Broadview Press Ltd, Peterborough, Ontario, 2001

Nadelhoffer, Hans. *Cartier*, Thames and Hudson, London, 2007

Phegley, Jennifer. *Courtship and Marriage in Victorian England*, Praeger, Santa Barbara, CA, 2012

Phillips, Clare (ed.). *Bejewelled by Tiffany 1837-1987*, Yale University Press, New Haven and London, 2006

Phillips, Clare. *Jewels and Jewellery*, Victoria and Albert Museum, London. Thames & Hudson, London, 2019

Proddow, Penny and Fasel, Marion. *With this Ring: The Ultimate Guide to Wedding Jewelry*, Bulfinch Press, New York, 2004

Roberts, Jane. *Five Gold Rings: A Royal Wedding Souvenir Album from Queen Victoria to Queen Elizabeth II*, Royal Collection Publications, London, 2007

Scarisbrick, Diana. *Le grand frisson bijoux de sentiment de la Renaissance à nos jours*, Chaumet, Paris. Les editions textuel, Paris, 2008

Scarisbrick, Diana. *Rings: Symbols of Wealth, Power and Affection*, Thames & Hudson, London, 1993

Scarisbrick, Diana. *Rings: Jewellery of Love, Power and Loyalty*, Thames & Hudson, London 2013

Schenke, Gesa. *Schein und Sein: Schmuckgebrauch in der Römischen Kaiserzeit*, Peeters, Louvain and Dudley, MA, 2003

Taylor, Elizabeth. *My Love Affair with Jewelry*, Thames and Hudson, London, 2002

Weir, Alison; Williams, Kate; Gristwood, Sarah and Borman, Tracy. *The Ring and the Crown: A History of Royal Weddings 1066-2011*, Hutchinson, London, 2011

Williams, Dyfri and Ogden, Jack. *Greek Gold: Jewellery of the Classical World*, British Museum Press, London, 1994

Picture Credits

© AGIP / Bridgeman Images fig. 6.26a
Agnolo Bronzino, National Gallery, Prague fig. 3.4
Alice and Louis Koch Collection in the Swiss National Museum, Zurich. Photo: Donat Stuppan figs. 1.4, 1.10, 1.13, 1.14, 1.18, 1.23, 2.5, 3.2, 3.3a, 3.3b, 3.8, 3.14, 3.22, 4.9, 4.12, 4.14a, 4.14b, 4.19, 4.22, 4.23, 4.24, 4.26a, 4.26b, 4.27, 4.28, 4.29, 5.6, 5.7, 5.10a, 5.10b, 5.11a 5.11b, 5.17a, 5.17b, 5.19, 5.20, 5.21, 5.22, 5.25, 6.10
© Annoushka Jewellery figs. 6.33a, 6.33 b
The Benjamin Zucker Family Collection Photo credit: R. Goodbody fig. 2.23
© Boodles fig. 6.50
© Boucher, Francois (1703-70) / Bridgeman Images fig.4.1

© BPK, Berlin, Dist. RMN-Grand Palais / Elke Estel / Hans-Peter Klut fig. 1.2
© BPK, Kunstgewerbemuseum, SMB fig. 2.1
Bridgeman Images figs. 1.9, 1.12, 2.4, 2.20, 3.13, 3.25a, 3.25b, 3.31, 4.15, 6.14, 6.25b
Brigitte Stefan TLDA Weimar fig. 2.9
© The Trustees of the British Museum figs. 1.1, 1.5, 1.6, 1.16, 2.6, 2.11, 2.19, 2.24, 5.14, 2.3, 2.15, 2.16
© Cartier figs. 6.1, 6.2a, 6.2b
© Chaumet, Paris figs. 6.34, 6.3, 6.4, 6.6, 5.16
Chip Clark and digitally enhanced by SquareMoose provided courtesy of the Smithsonian Institution fig. 5.4
© Christies fig. 6.49
Christopher Polk / Getty Images fig. 6.48

Created by Cosway, Richard (1742-1821) (after) / Bridgeman Images fig. 4.30
De Agostini Picture Library / A. Dagli Orti / Bridgeman Images figs. 3.16, 3.18
De Agostini Picture Library / L. Douglas / Bridgeman Images fig. 5.5
© Dennis Stock/Magnum Photos fig. 6.21
© Dist. RMN-Grand Palais / Martine Beck-Coppola fig. 4.7
Everett Collection / Bridgeman Images fig. 6.41
© Fabio Salini figs. 6.32a, 6.32b
Fol. 249v. Codex Manesse (ca.1300). / Bridgeman Images fig. 2.2
© Gerd Rothmann / Owner: M. Pollack and H Huth, Hudson, N.Y. fig. 6.53

Acknowledgements

This book is the result of the contributions and efforts of so many different people from across all aspects of jewellery. *The Power of Love* is all the richer for their collective involvement and experience.

I am especially indebted to the Alice and Louis Koch Foundation for allowing us to feature so many of their wonderful rings from its private collection courtesy of the Swiss National Museum in Zurich. My sincere thanks also go to Sandra Hindman and her lovely team at Les Enluminures, and Benjamin Zucker for their continuing support and expertise. To the team at Unicorn Publishing - Lucy Duckworth, Editorial Director and Felicity Price-Smith, Designer and Sophie Lee, the copy editor who has tirelessly checked and proofed every date, jewel and text, my immense gratitude.

Finally, my great thanks to all the friends, jewellers, designers and colleagues who generously contributed to the story of *The Power of Love - Jewels, Romance and Eternity*: Annoushka, Boodles, Bulgari, Cartier, Chaumet, Diana Scarisbrick, Fabio Salini, Garrard, Gerd Rothmann, Ilgiz Fazulyanov, Jane Sarginson, Maria Stürzebecher (Erfurt), Mikimoto, Nancy & David Skier, Niessing, Otto Künzli, Palais Princier de Monaco, Shaun Leane, SJ Philips, Smithsonian Institute, Solange Azagury-Partridge, Stephen Webster, Tadema Gallery, Tiffany & Co., Van Cleef & Arpels, Wallace Chan and Wartski.

My special thanks go to Lord Strathcarron, Chairman Unicorn Publishing Group for having the inspiration to publish this wonderful book following a conversation with accomplished jewellery photographer, Paul Hartley and ex-De Beers executive, Fiona Spence. I was delighted to be asked to author *The Power of Love*.

First published by Unicorn
an imprint of Unicorn Publishing Group LLP, 2019
5 Newburgh Street
London W1F 7RG
www.unicornpublishing.org

This publication is partially funded with financial support
from Les Enluminures LTD and Benjamin Zucker.

10 9 8 7 6 5 4 3 2 1

ISBN 978-1-911604-46-4

Jacket illustrations
Front: Pendant with Cupid and Billing Doves (detail, see fig. 3.20)
Back: Heart-shaped ring with Lover's Eye (see fig. 4.31)

Managing Editor: Fiona Spence
Copy-editor: Sophie Lee
Designed by Felicity Price-Smith
Printed by Imprint Press